The Poetess

BLAIR SMITH

The Poetesses: Abigirl Phiri - Blessing Adebola - Caitlin Wilcox - Claire Deakin - Comfort Japheth Ebzan - Dana Michele Sheehy - Dahlia Constant - Heather Harris - Lavin Owende - Maria Aparecida Guimaraes - Michelle Cintron - Obiora Precious - Oceana Lushay Smith - Pamela Atieno Omondi - Ranjana Rai - Rose R. Sales - Ruth Namatovu - Sali Andiamo Siyaya - Sarah Otieno - Somdatta Mitra - Ula Douglas

Printed in the United States of America

ISBN: 979-8-8693-8807-0

10 9 8 7 6 5 4 3 2 1

EMPIRE PUBLISHING
www.empirebookpublishing.com

DEDICATION

This book is dedicated to the poetess. For centuries the poetess was only known as "Anonymous". For most of history, women were not supposed to be writers, poets, or many other things except their traditional roles. This collection of work from 21 beautiful poetesses gives their voice a larger platform to be heard by even more people. Their collective voices from around the world are brought together in this book to honor the poetess.

"If there ever was a voice missing from the world's most important conversations about war, religion, politics, education, and healthcare, it would be the voice of the poetess. "

-Blair Smith

FORWARD

"The Poetess" first started out as idea born sometime around January 2020 just before the world experienced the Covid-19 pandemic. In early days, I sought out to promote a World Poetry book, but after a change of heart, what I really wanted to do first was to honor the poetess, promote their work and provide a larger platform for the most deserving.

It has been said that your power is not your true power unless you give it away. After publishing my own book in 2018, I had learned the publishing process and what I needed to do to help promote others. "The Poetess" reflects those lessons learned and has taught me new lessons in promoting a book.

The selected poetesses are from Brazil, Spain, India, Puerto Rico, Nigeria, Philippines, Zimbabwe, Kenya, Bhutan, Malawi, Uganda, the UK, and the US. They range in age from 17 to 77 years old. The common thread binding all of them is their passion for poetry.

The criteria for the selectees were unique in that we were not looking for the already famous, well known or the widely published. We wanted the "up and comers" with the potential to be great! We selected those who expressed passion in their work much like a singer owning their song. Other criteria included a poetess who gives her poetry a strong, confident voice with poetic expression. All selectees were interviewed over Zoom by the editor Theo Clement and me the promoter Blair Smith.

By providing a larger stage for the selectees, I experienced giving away my own journey while empowering others. Many of the selectees may not have otherwise been published on Amazon or had their poetry put into a book. In a larger sense, "The Poetess" promotes positive ripples into the universe by way of providing a source of positivity to the selectee's family, friends and associates who will now see them as a credible, published writer. Additionally, instead of a scattered picture of a smile left behind on some future family member's hallway- their names will live on, and future family members may get to know them through their writings long after they are gone. Ladies and gentlemen, it is my pleasure to present to you "The Poetess."

-Blair Smith

Table of Contents

CHAPTER FOURTEEN: ABIGIRL PHIRI

CHAPTER FIFTEEN: PAMELA ATIENO OMONDI (PAMWRITES)

CHAPTER EIGHTEEN: SALI ANDIAMO SIYAYA

CHAPTER NINETEEN: DANA MICHELE SHEEHY

HEATHER E. HARRIS

AGE: 44

HOME TOWN: HENDERSON, NV

COUNTRY: UNITED STATES

WHY DO YOU WRITE POETRY?

I write as a form of expression, to share my thoughts, to inspire others to share theirs. We all experience challenges in life and moments to celebrate. We are all unique and different, at the same time we are all one.

WHY IS YOU MESSAGE TO THE WORLD?

I want to bring peace, comfort and unconditional love to the world. Everyone matters. Everyone is important. Everyone deserves to be loved. Together we can heal the world and bring forth more joy and happiness.

CHAPTER ONE
HEATHER E. HARRIS

MIND AND HEART

My mind is blank, I cannot see.
The pain in my heart is blocking me.
My mind and heart connect as one.
When will I feel warmth from the sun?

Heather Harris

Dedicated to Blair Smith for his courage to give me honest feedback and support to open up, be vulnerable and heal. I appreciate you!

INVISIBLE

I thought I was invincible
I'm strong, nothing can touch me.
I decide how I feel.

That day changed everything.
I didn't know. How could this be?
I looked, is that you before my eyes?
No, but still I feel.

That day I watched you struggle in pain.
You died right before my eyes.
For you the pain was finally over.
For me, it's pain I always feel.

It wasn't you; it was someone else.
It was someone who looked a lot like you.
The man was a complete stranger to me.
The pain of loss I forever feel.

Heather Harris

Author's Note: Each time I read this or think about the moment, my eyes feel with tears and I cry. I may be a nurse, but I also have a heart just like everyone else and experience emotions. I feel. I'm not invincible.

Dedicated to everyone who has ever lost someone. May you find everlasting peace and comfort.

HEART BROKEN

I start each morning thinking of you,
Your smile, your laugh, your touch.

I wonder what could have been,
If you had only given me a chance.

My heart was a gift you did not want,
My love too strong and intense.

I'm not mad, just sad and heart broken.
For you I only want the best.

These eyes have cried the last tears.
For me I only want the best.

My heart is strong, it will go on.
With love, no longer heart broken.

Heather Harris

Dedicated to my friend Jan Thomason Bollendorf for her courage to allow her heart to heal and grow in love.

LIFE

Sometimes I just feel helpless.
I don't know what to think.
I don't know how to feel.
I don't know what to do.
I don't know where to go.

I want to belong.
I want to be loved.
I want to be cherished.
I want to be cared for.
I want to be appreciated.

Where do I start?
How do I decide?
What does it look like?
Why does it matter?
Where do I go from here?

The choice is set before me.
Will I be a victim or a leader?
Will I shine or fade?
Will I succeed or fail?
Will I grow or whither?

In the end, the choice is simple,
The path of my life is up to me.

Heather Harris

Dedicated to my sons Landen and Cade Harris for standing by me on this rollercoaster called life. Your path is up to you. Choose wisely and have no regrets.

MY WANTED MAN

I want a man who loves me,
Who is always thinking of me.

I want a man who protects me,
Who likes to keep me safe.

I want a man who rescues me,
Who is always there when I need him.

I want a man who prioritizes me,
Who enjoys spending time with me.

aI want a man as my best friend,
Who shares with me all of his dreams.

I want a man who wants me,
Who can't imagine his life without me.

My wanted man I'm ready for you,
Come find me as fast as you can.

Heather Harris

Author's Note: I'm often asked what I look for in a man. Here is my list.

Dedicated to Elizabeth Jeser and Nancy Whissel for teaching me it is just as important to receive as it is to give and I'm worth it always!

MY LOVE

My love for you is like the ocean,
Vast, strong, deep, never ending.

On good days and bad days,
It is always there, ready to surround you.

No current too strong or obstacle too great,
To ever weaken, deter or stop it.

I know some days you say it's too much,
You say you don't deserve it.

I must say that you are wrong!
You deserve all of it and more!

You are worth it always.
You are my love.

Heather Harris

Author's Note: This poem is about unconditional love. To be able to love someone with all my heart, no conditions, I had to first learn to love myself. Before I learned to love myself there were times, I did not feel like I was worth loving. Now I radiate love and enjoy sharing the warmth.

Dedicated to Madison Beatty who lives each day as the ultimate example of unconditional love.

GOOD BYE

Today is the day I must go.
I must collect my things and leave.
I'm not wanted by you anymore.

Tears of sadness run down my face.
I can't take it anymore.
The hurt and pain I feel is too great!

Good bye my love.

Heather Harris

Dedicated to everyone who has the courage to leave an unhealthy relationship. You are enough, just as you are! You are worth it!

A GIFT

Take a walk with me.

Hold my hand.

Look deeply into my eyes.

Let me know with a simple glance,

How much I mean to you.

Today is a gift I am grateful to have.

Tomorrow is a present I look forward to.

Heather Harris

Dedicated to my grandma Marian DeLapp Woolsey who always held my hand and was there when I needed her most.

BROKEN

Broken mirror, shattered glass
My reflection all around me.

Who is this broken woman I see?
Is this who I want to be?

Scattered thoughts, restless mind,
What is it I really want?

I close my eyes and count to ten.
My eyes open and there I am.

Shattered mirror broken no more,
A beautiful, complete woman I see.

She was present, there all along.
All I had to do was believe.

Heather Harris

Dedicated to my best friend Yolanda Kruhaj for always believing in me and supporting me every step of the way.
I wouldn't be where I am today without her.

EACH TIME

Each time I think of you I smile
My heart beats faster
My body fills with warmth
I experience happiness and joy.

Each time I see you I'm home.
I want to be held by your arms.
I want to feel your heart beat.
I'm right where I belong.

Each time I dream of you I'm open,
Open to possibilities of what may be
Open to the present and how it is
Open to the future and how it may be

All I want for you is a life of
Joy, love, family and happiness.
You mean everything to me.

Heather Harris

Dedicated to my friend Dr. Teddy Sim. May you one day find again the love of your life. You deserve the best!

SIGNS

Signs all around me telling me where to go,
Which do I follow?
How do I know?

Distraction and (versus Distractors) warnings all around,
How do I see past them?
How do I know what is real?

Confused, undecided, which way to go,
What is my true path?
What is my destiny?

No more waiting, It's decision time!

Heather Harris

Author's Note: This poem is about intuition. Society teaches us that we need tangible evidence to follow in every decision, but that is not always the case. Sometimes we get a feeling or inner knowing of an action to take or path to follow that makes sense only to us. We either trust ourselves and do what we know to be true, or surrender to societal pressure and fear and doubt ourselves. Either way, the choice is up to us.

Dedicated to anyone who struggles with following their intuition and knowing that they are worth it.

JUST ME

I've always tried to be who you wanted me to be.
Accept me. Love me. Want me.

I sacrifice everything for you.
Accept me. Love me. Want me.

I share with you all of my private thoughts.
Accept me. Love me. Want me.

You hide yourself from me.
Accept me. Love me. Want me.

You hurt me more than you'll ever know.
Accept me. Love me. Want me.

It's time for me to let go.
I accept me. I love me. I want me.

It's time to value myself more.
I accept me. I love me. I want me.

It's time to see all of the beauty inside of me.
I accept me. I love me. I want me.

It's time to accept both the light and dark.
I accept me. I love me. I want me.

It's time to accept all of me.
I accept me. I love me. I want me.

It's time to just be me.

Heather Harris

Dedicated to my sister Nicole Hope. May you one day see and realize that you are enough, just as you are.

DARK AND LIGHT

In the darkness there is a light,
It may grow or become extinguished;
the choice is yours.

Will you allow the darkness to overcome you,
To fill your body and soul with sadness?

Will you allow the light to grow,
To become brighter with every moment and give hope?

In the end it is a simple choice,
Darkness or light, which will you choose?

Heather Harris

Dedicated to my friend Dr. Landon Poppleton for constantly listening, teaching me and always accepting me just as I am

MY BEST FRIEND

He's the kindest man I know.
Has a heart of gold.
Sacrifices more than he should.
Deserves more than he knows.
I hope he knows I understand,
Sometimes life deals a bad hand.
Always beside him I will stand.
Grateful and blessed am I
To always trust this man.

Heather Harris

Dedicated to my best friend Macario Gallegos, Jr. for always believing in me and my potential. Trusting him and embarking on this emotional intelligence journey is one of the best decisions I have ever made.

SOMDATTA MITRA

COUNTRY: INDIA

WHY DO YOU WRITE POETRY?

Well, I write poetry because it gives me a sense of individuality, it's a mirror to identify that freedom to explore thoughts. It empowers my personality as an independent thinker and enhances my spirit to worship literature.

WHAT IS YOUR MESSAGE TO THE WORLD?

My message to the world is that Poetry suffices all voids. And the more we are enriched with good moralities; we can imbue it to the next generation for a healthy thinking. Poetry adorns that thought process with a natural and dulcet tones. So, through poetry unite for a world friendship to beautify this world and propagate love.

CHAPTER TWO
SOMDATTA MITRA

PEACE

With tolerance as we forgive,
Those malpractices or malice which stings.
Where the wings spread to fly high,
To reach a destination to glorify.
Peace nest in each heart to simply embrace life,
Harmony beautifies each smile to unite hearts to sing.

In a serendipity often festivals unite all,
Jubilations galore to enchant.
Divine perspectives embellish the solemn heart,
And enthuse passion to a beatitude.
Peace is an ornament to an inborn right,
Where each heart beats for an authentic joy ride.

Where the squeals of misery and poverty are cradled,
With sufficient care and concern.
Where the enthusiasm to cherish the rights with dignity,
Never suppress the innocence with inhumanity.
Peace dwells in nook and corner,
Of each mind as an adorner.

CHRISTMAS FOR THE UNFED

Assuming the prerogatives,
Of the arrival of Santa in our lives.
Who share happiness, cheer and laughter,
In a delight and mesmerize.

The whole world is configuring a phase,
Where food and shelter are most essential that is acclaimed.
Twice a day's meal to each and every individual,
Will be the best Christmas gift to adhere.

With abundant love and affection, we all expect,
An upliftment of humanity while embracing
peace and tranquility over evil means.

The moments of corruption, malpractices, cheating and hypocrisy,
And ravenous means must be a cognizant
to surpass the social evils.
For a convivial atmosphere in a disparate world of thoughts,
We need to construe alacrity in a camaraderie.

To get rid of blandishment and beguile intents,
We must release honesty from a camouflage.
A sense of compassion, empathy and concern can transform,
All the malice, avarice and covetousness to a magical world.

That loathsome, diabolical moments shall be erased,
With Santa's sweet snigger.
Just like the pious moment of the birth of Jesus Christ,
I dream of a moment when a child is born in 21st century.
To bring a renaissance and loud cheer,
To emboss love for peace in a deferential manner.

I'M YOUR PEN
AND WILL YOU BE MY POETRY?

With elegance I spread the ink in a paper,
To embellish words to construct deep emotions like a painter.
With each line I try to uplift the exuberance,
As the experiences I portray with my deep intellect.

At times the ink imbues my thirst to be humorous,
Melancholy and mourning reflect through the similes
and personification.
In a scornful expression at times I rebel against destiny,
When a patient suffering from cancer;
Is treated with coumarins at large with empathy.

Life means so much of beautiful things to cherish,
Hey! with my fragrance, admirance and love
can you be my poetry and unleash?

With innumerable ideas I assemble the passion and intensify,
With variance I try to connect to hearts for perspective and justify.
Love the different feelings to gather in one envelope,
As the conviction to create a beautiful piece;
Attracts me in my own kaleidoscope.

The ink that flows from inside my heart,
Gathers so many excitements,
desires or divine pleasure in a jumpstart.
From angels to witches I scale high with poetic devices,
From mountains to rivers,
I float easily through my sarcasm or idioms with suffices.

How diligent I'm to integrate wonderful words or phrases!
With my nib I want to create an ode to you, my dearest.

To enrich lives with you my poetry,
Let me be the poet in a parody.
Let love and passion reach heights of emotional amalgamation,
Let the poets enjoy my spirit to witness
the blossoming of my temptation.

While I bow down to propose for a union,
Will you be my poetry as a poet I extend my hand?

INSTA ID: mitrasomdatta

THE SHINING STARS INVADE OUR HEARTS

With one wink as I witness the twinkling stars,
My soul is purified with the glimmer.
Their brightness impacts our mind,
It calms us over depressions and anxieties being so kind.
With the vivacity they reign in the sky,
Their names are often called by the scientists with a loud cry.
The child sleeps in a divine bliss,
The moonlit night transcends all the peripheries.
That refulgence and radiance increase more attraction,
The lovers are in a glorious sensitivity to attract
Cupid in a confession.

The eagerness of the night,
To envelope all in love on Christmas is a divine blessing.
The carriage passing by the woods stop for a while,
Astounded the passengers cherish those splendid moments.

Happiness gathers in each and every person's heart,
As the coachman smiles.
Enlivening the lives of all, the shining stars instill a solace.
That it was time for merriment,
The families gather to embrace.

In a solitary refinement the priests tend to appeal,
the religious nuns for a prelude.
It is time for the birth of the holy Lord,
Jingle bells Jingle bells echoes in each heart.

Bethlehem receives fervor,
Celebrations surmount in the nook and corner.
Shining brightly the stars dazzle and emblazon,
The holy night and enthuse a spirit of spiritual bliss.

In a harmonic and benevolent spirit,
The whole world is enveloped in a sensitivity.
To welcome Jesus our savior,
To emboss peace and sanctity.

IF I COULD BE A DOLL AND SHARE SMILES:

Wallowing in depression the waifs scream in a nemesis,
Unable to express their misery with much emphasis.
If I could be a doll to raise their innocent smiles,
Holding me tight they would embrace;
In a yagiment.
I would be an apple of their eye in an umbworld,
I would rejoice over a union in their abode.
Their radiant smile would enliven my heart,
My attractive appearance perhaps,
Would enthuse a contentment in a HeadStart.

So divine will be my pleasure,
To enjoy a few moments in this disguise.
That a glimpse of those cheerful faces,
Will simply ameliorates with a temptation.
Their integrity and purity will bedizen their souls in a jollity,
With me over their chest to play;
A beautiful world will kalong in an exasperation.
If I could be a doll and share smiles,
I would be sparkling sensation to attract;
Those despondent ragamuffins in a delight.
I want to be their glorious smiles,
And chase their innocence to intensify their exhilaration.

IN A SOLITITUDE

Like a maverick I want to enthuse passion,
A moment of infatuation like an inflorescence to be indulgent.
Felicitous over our togetherness in this holy night,
As the stars twinkle as if to greet us in a delight.
Let us embrace each other enveloped in love,
And wrap this quilt to be close to each other;
In a solicitude and settle in virtue of.
Let this fire ignite the sensations and deep
excitement like a concupiscent,
Let your fragrance instill promiscuous felicity
in an evangelical ardor.
Worshipping our togetherness in a falsetto,
I feel like I'm in the seventh heaven in this midnight.

You being my integral part of life,
Churning my emotions towards an insane
edelweiss in an effusion.
Let this eerie feeling gallop towards an edifice of love,
Where we both will correspond with each other and comprehend.
In this spiritual union of two hearts,
I was besieged by Cupid and his comrades
to embellish you my lady love.
With unending poems,
ballads or sonnets throughout this beautiful night,
Where the stars are winking as if to tease our belonging
in an emprise.
The more you shower love with your deep breath,
The more my composure makes me a hostage
of this vehement passion.
As if an obstreperous heart obviates the random urge to be free,
And liberate our souls to unite in any degree.

Insta id: mitrasomdatta

LET ME HUG YOU MY PRECOCIOUS WHELP

Singing cantabile like an obsessed mother,
Cradling you over and over again and cosseted.
As a baby you enjoyed those mollycoddles wearing a bonnet,
How stupefying those moments of joy which you gifted me!
As a mother your divine squeaks enhanced my spirits in a glee.
As you grew up to be a teenager in recent years,
A mother's heart always longed for those coddles in a cheer.
An insistence on gifting me a wonderful hug
with your sincere warmth,
On Mother's Day you deliberately consummate
a sensational interview of mine.

Over our rooftop it was accomplished
with meticulous perspective,
Where I confronted you as a guest of " COFFEE WITH SRINJOY "
in a magnificent camaraderie.
Hugging a coffee mug for some appealing pictures,
Your astute presentation of the chat show
flabbergasted my conscience.
Like a debonair your constant queries,
Established a situation of real thrill
like a television show in a reality.
I was in the seventh heaven to perceive,
That I was an important personality to repertoire.
With a warm embrace you adorned me
with a Mother's Day crown,
As a handcrafted career you embellished it
to a blissful endowment.
Reminiscences of those glorious moments here I cherish,
On HUGS DAY the resonances of your kvetch;
As a baby triggers my sensations.
Let me hug you my precocious whelp,
With innumerable aspirations may you succeed in life I bless.

SMILES ENRICH EMOTIONS

Cheerful faces engender passion and admiration,
Encouraging a vivify contentment to be refreshful.
Always smiling with a gleeful expression,
Gracefully ornaments our countenance.

Often, we witness people with vainglory,
They lose charm on their faces over a discriminatory.
Restraining a simple smile seems appearing in an examination,
My reflections over this crisis,
In our society requires a dissociation.

In the name of an egalitarian society,
There are discriminations that become a mound.
I have witnessed the eunuchs are subjected to fear,
Their obstreperous actions often trigger criticisms.
Unknown and unaware of their lost smiles,
They encage themselves in a shell without any expression.
Nonplussed by their enigma,
one tends to envelope in a bad impression.

To heal the depressants and the insecure,
To comfort those who are mourning and destined to suffer.
A sweet, genial smile is often a healer,
A happiness that can be gifted to everyone without any cost.

LIMERENCE

Apathy to liberate the veiled desires,
Capri ant spirits dig the infatuation.
Troubled, perplexed mind tingle perturbation,
Cogitating the anxious queries.

Unconditional and eternal cravings subjugate,
Redefining a sensitivity for a canoodle.
Augmenting to a Kairos,
Love blossoms into a dalliance.

Vociferous expressions enjoin the innocent lambkins,
Amorousness blithely consent traboccant romances

©®Somdatta Mitra

UNITY IN DIVERSITY

Unfathomed arenas of diverse cultures and heritage,
Yet strongly raising a voice of unity as a desideratum.
Our country is indoctrinated over harmony,
And the different languages and religions ensconce in a Eugenie.

Loud and free they yell with a proud cheer,
Singing the national anthem unitedly in a sprightful atmosphere.
That coadunation of a thunderous acclamation,
That our country is the best in the world.

Adulating the diversity in religions, cultures,
languages and heritage,
Unity adorns their real existence even in wars.
Sacrificing lives for their country and guarding the nation,
There is no discrimination over the emotion of "being an Indian".
Nation comes first and then the family,
Together they are audacious and bold to squeak
"Vande Mataram".

Like a rainbow they parade in a queue,
Salute the martyrs as the gallantry awards coronet
the Bravehearts as a taboo.
Jai Hind is their slogan to enrich life,
Their pride of being one is the soulfulness.

EXPLORE THE CHILD WITHIN YOU

If you are a wanderer in the journey of life,
Never bother what others feel for you in a stride.
Living for self-satisfaction,
Is the primary need to enjoy a bliss.
Be a child at times to remind yourself a time,
That you have already passed and grew.

If you are an adventurer amidst the commotion,
Search for a place of seclusion to give a new definition.
There you play for hours like a child with toys,
That you feel you won't hide from others.
Be a child at times to rejoice over the soulful moments,
That gift you with such abundant treasures.

If you are a player in your life,
Learn to be a game changer in a drive.
Every secured cheerfulness while you play with the children,
Will be an album of high spirits with naughtiness.
While you unravel the paths of distance,
The child within you;
Seem to mesmerize for a plan to settle in this paradise.

EXPECTATIONS ON NEW YEAR

Radiated to renew,
It seems time spreads its wings to review.
A year passing with grievances and excitements,
With gallery of incidents and experiences.

Eclectic vibes in an egalitarian society,
Lost affection blended with pretentious smiles,
in an insobriety.
Tough to battle the subtility,
Easy to embrace in a cordiality.

Resolving and again surrendering to subjugation,
Deliberate impulse echo for a reformation.
Love yourself and mirror the ridges,
Fearlessly vociferate the injustices and wrongs.
Honest commitments must be adhered,
Unconditional love must not be confused with expectations.

Paramount essence of freedom,
Wallowing in the bond of relations to a naivete like a combretum.
New year resolutions must bring new aspirations,
New year 2024 shines brightly for a desire to host.
A paraphernalia to construct a paradise of understanding,
Where souls receive bliss that will remain everlasting.

©®Somdatta Mitra

THAT SUBTLE SMILE

I cherish the words of the pauper who smiled at me,
When the loud cheer of the children unbolted a victory.
Over his hidden emotions,
I was somewhat hesitant to unleash my feelings.

Yet I felt a kind of grin,
As the bus trespassed the yards.
The bright moss roses enjoined a divinity over blossoming,
The Sun enriched our spirits as if to welcome over homecoming.

Fifteen days of stay in a farm,
For the holidays that we planned to affirm.
My father 's best friend's invitation,
Finally gifted some hidden treasures.

How meticulous their family were to govern a hospitality!
How stupefying the nature was over the high mountains!
The lambs emboldened as the grazing time legitimated,
The sunflowers winked as if to remind me of that pauper.

Yes, his smile was subtle,
To remind me that life bestows beauty and melancholy.
To learn how to embrace life,
And endeavor to be always happy even in adversities.

BLOSSOM WITH PURITY

Blossom with purity,
Spray the fragrance with divinity.
Bloom and thrive with simplicity,
Be a flower which is symbolic of real beauty.

Unfold expressions of love and peace with sincerity,
Embrace the soil affectionately.
Bow down to the soil infinitely,
And take a vow to fertile it with your fragrance.

Be a flower and expand your petals,
Grow for the strength and dignity to edulcorate harmony.
Dive into the holy admirance of beatitude,
And admire the optimism in nurturing.

Your gardener must imbue the determination for your goals,
And he must sprinkle some confidence and courage to rise in the sunshine.
Be bold and charismatic like a flower,
With the essence of an aplomb.

When your stem is strong enough to stand firm,
Be like a flower to bestow pleasure to all around you.
Mitigate the sufferings of misery,
Through your beauty and fragrance.

Cheer up those,
Who are compelled to breathe in adversities.

With your innate positive vibes,
Lend your perfection to cradle their hearts;
And relieve them from the troubles and melancholy.

Be a flower to touch the gentle breeze with mirth,
With each gaze enjoy the serenity and bliss.
Let the Sun engender pride,
With your flamboyance the world will be astonished!

©® Somdatta Mitra

MOMENTS THAT BLOSSOMED LOVE

Bombinating the epiphany of our first rendezvous,
Expressions were numb over a passionate delectation.
Unaware of the persistent infatuation and delirium,
Our course of attraction aggrandized
the heartbeats in an imperium.

Over the bridge as we sauntered in an oblivion,
The dark night regaled in a caution.
The lamp posts whisked off the blooming sensuousness,
Amidst the seclusion and the perpetual pleasure.

Striking together in a haste,
I reminiscence our first meet in the college.
So, Elysium was love at first sight,
The ambivalent reciprocation aureate to a divinity.

A beau gets to console me over a catastrophe,
A propinquity over the emotional comfort escalated a craze.
We dived into a preponderance in this demesne,
Life without each other was impossible.

Impassive and impatient we chased the moments of desperation,
Benumbed in that snowy night as an exploration.
Holding each other in an emollient elucidation.

CLAIRE DEAKIN (*DREAM WEAVER*)

COUNTRY: ENGLAND (*MANCETTER*)

ABOUT ME CLAIRE DEAKEN © DREAMWEAVER

Hello my name is Claire Deakin, I'm 43 years old. I live in a small village just outside a little market town in Mancetter. In the UK. I'm married to my husband and have four children.

Since having to take early retirement at the end of the pandemic due to ill health, back in 2022 I found myself having too much time on my hands. So, I started spending my time listening to music and writing poetry. Little did I know that one poem would change the course of my life in the future. I'm a huge Sam Ryder fan, who's a British singer/songwriter and voice actor, so I just wrote a short poem and tagged him in it online in September 2022. I was shocked when I received a private message from him, thanking me for the poem. We became online friends. He's my idol and biggest inspiration behind the beginning of my poetic journey. He encouraged me to follow my dreams, which was to become a published author. A dream that I had nearly all but given up on. I regularly share my work with him.

I write my poetry as a way of expressing my inner most thoughts and feelings. As well as to paint a picture for readers to be drawn into. Each piece is unique and can pinpoint a pinnacle life event and feelings as they are directly linked. I write what I feel in the moment. My collection grew. Having a range of genre of poetry, broadened the audience.

Over this past year and a half, my poems have received so many positive and, in some cases, an emotional response. They were bringing joy and hope to those that were struggling in life. As a Christian, I felt as though I had received my calling from God. I became a beacon of hope and light.

My life's journey has been an emotional one. I found inspiration and comfort in the unlikeliest of places and people. It was emotional for to see my poetry out there. I didn't realize until recently, that my unique experience and perception of life just how relatable or inspiring my words were to others. I didn't know that I shared a similar voice and message with so many people or that my ability to empathize with them would fuel my writing. Resonating on a spiritual level across all genres.

I continue to write, as a way of expressing myself, my love, feelings and empathy in the hope of connecting with people. With having a positive and realistic approach to looking at life. A message of reassurance or divine intervention from God or a flutter in my heart.

CHAPTER THREE
CLAIRE DEAKIN (DREAM WEAVER)

A MORTAL SOUL

I am all but a mortal soul, who wants to
share this moment like no other.
A love like mine can melt the heart,
A love so strong it will never be torn apart.
I long to hold my significant other, but there are
so many, I can't tell one from the other.
When things go wrong, as they sometimes will,
When every road you take, is always up hill.
When funds are low, and debts are high,
Always try to smile, instead of letting out a sigh.
Keep pressing on and rest a while, when you stop
For surely with perseverance, you will reach the top.
For mortals like you and me, can be whatever we inspire to be.

ALONG OUR TRAVELS AWAY

Travelling along we go, always stopping or about to go. The cars, the traffic, the views of place as we drive by, it would be quicker to be a bird and fly. Oh, how I wish I was a bird flying free. Nothing but the great blue sky. Instead, I'm sitting here, needing to go far but having to stay near. I want to reach my destination, not sit here for the whole duration.

I'm going somewhere I have been before but the views as we drive, make me feel like we're never going to arrive. The view goes by as slow as time, for we're hitting traffic every road we turn. Sitting here with nothing but time to burn. At last, we pick up pace, we're cruising along not in a race.

The cars, the trees they all fly pass, even though we are not going fast. We navigate, lane by lane, until we can get into one, we can remain. We go South to head across West, not knowing which way is best.

As time goes by, I sit and wonder why the music plays, as I write as I have little words to say out loud, for they are all in my mind. As we settle at a steady pace, I sit and bask with the sun on my face.

Music playing in the background on low, many more miles still to go. The scenery is continuously on the change, as we set the course to stay in the right speed range.

I recognize the cars, some passing but never getting far. We drive along the winding road; our final destination is known. Fields and hills either side, I sit back and enjoy the ride.

As we drive through Cyramu, there is a breath-taking beautiful view. I'm glad I'm on this journey with. I can no longer read the signs, for they are going from English to Welsh. So, of the hardest words I'll ever try and pronounce.

12 miles or so, along this road we still must go. Counting down the junctions, getting us there is the cars only function. Listening to the radio, onwards and upwards we must go.

The valleys are steep, the hills are high. The scenery is changing vastly as we drive by. Navigating through this foreign land, with nothing else but a pen in my hand. Writing during this journey, helps keep my mind focused and busy.

With a little over an hour to go, I continue to look out through the window. It's all I can do but sit and laugh as to my disbelief a man is on a scooter. His feet pushing him along in a very strange and peculiar way. With the wind in his hair, I wonder how long it will take for him to get there.

I can tell we're in Wales, for just as the hills are steep, they are also like home for the sheep. In my line of view, I keep them, for surely trying count them one by one, would take far too long.

The last half an hour we must remain focused and strong, now is not the time for things to go wrong. As we begin to tire and our muscles ache, the last leg of this journey we must take.

Not much further to go, before we get to rest. I'm proud of my companion for he is the best. For today he surely has passed the test.

CHAT POETRY

(Me)

"I hold your hand"

I absolutely love, to hold your hand at night,
If I'm having a bad dream, it seems to make it right.
When you toss and turn, your hand slips away,
But then we reunite, and everything's okay.

(Him)

When you hold my hand, and whisper sweet things.
Know that your loving touch, pulls at my heart strings.
And when you're next to me, life is just divine,
Walking into the sunset, with your hand in mine.

(Me)

Taking walks with you, strolling hand in hand,
A simple show of love, that we understand.
And when we stop our steps, your lips I do kiss,
I'll always hold your hand; I promise you this.

DEEP INTO YOUR EYES

Staring at this depressing screen,
only makes me tired and weak.
My soul is lost and my heart is bleak
How could life feel so mean.

I'd rather stare into your eyes.
Your eyes brighten up the sky in my mind.
They give me hope and light,
Making it difficult to cry.

The glint in them means everything's alright.
Your eyes hold 1000 oceans,
Enough for you to absorb all my emotions.
Your melancholic eyes,

Make feel I could reach for the skies.
Your eyes stir up feelings, not been felt in a while.
I'm captivated by your smile.
They say hello, believe them if you try.

The more I stare into your eyes,
The more I want more of you.
Your Angelic spirit captures mine,
In the deep cool moonlight.
Your eyes I find love so divine.
I delight in watching the flickering candle light.
How can your eyes make me feel all this,
I feel so alive, gazing deep into your eyes.

FORBIIDDEN LOVE

Have you ever been in love with a person, strictly in a platonic way. I'm trying to understand what you mean, by the words you convey.

All that are heart felt but remain unspoken between us.

Please feel free to talk, just so I can feel I'm not alone by myself in this situation, having a single sided conversation.

That's sweet you call me by my name. May it forever be always on the tip of your tongue.

As you continue to luster and long, long for the connection to be made and to become complete. Happy knowing that you have solely swept me clear off my feet.

The words flow through my mind onto paper. For our conversations and our friendship are the inspiration I favor.

Call it fate, call it cosmic. I believe it's the universe working its magic.

Taking to you is like a comfy pair of shoes. You can sit and feel warm and relaxed and never fear of being axed.

We can laugh and smile and chat for quite a while.

Walking hand in hand, barefoot across the sand.

For who could have known, that I could have would have fallen so completely and utterly in love with you.

My Centre a heart that beats with pace, left or right defines your grace.

Hedging my bets, that you'll know where I am. I'm your Dream Weaver author and your #1 fan. I'll be waiting for you to succeed in every way you can.

Talking to you is like a taking a gulp of fresh air. Whisk me away, I don't mind anywhere.

As long as I'm with you, there is no place I'd rather be, than right beside you in everything you do.

© Claire Deakin # Dream Weaver.

FREE SPIRIT

An independent person, who thinks for themselves. And rarely conform to society. They are quite optimistic lovers, who fight for what they believe. A fierce friend to have indeed. They're intuitive and comfortable in their own skin. And have a smile that shines from deep within.

Sweet Dreams Valentine.

Close your eyes, touch your heart.

Make a wish, from the very start.

Let it be known, darling that you don't

Have to be whole, in order to shine.

Kneel and pray and look up to the moon

And stars, for a soulful love so divine.

Everyone Needs a Hug.

A hug does so many things. It can bring joy and comfort, for those who get them. So, here's a hug, a gift from me to you. A special reminder that I'm thinking of you.

As you are someone special to me. You'll never have to beg for anything. Not my time, not my attention, not my love. For everything I give to you willingly, because loving you is killing me.

INSPIRATION

My inspiration came from those people in life
that showed me how to deal with love and strife.
My dreams of becoming big, I take step by step
Only getting closer with every footstep.
For their inspirations
fill my life with anticipation.

In life we have our little moments of joy,
There are too many to mention.
Each one can brighten up you day
If only we stopped and paid enough attention.

I lost my fear and gained a life
A life full of highs and lows
How far up though nobody knows.

MY WORDS

There is not much to say, apart from my words can paint a picture in my mind.

My work depends on my mood. As I have said so many times before, nothing or anyone in particular inspires me.
My words just flow with ease through me.

No pretense, these are my words as they tumble through my mind. Until pen to paper do I find.

I am happy standing in the shadows of my words.

Instead of trying to shine because my inner light, is not so bright.

I let my words tell you, my story. As I don't like to let people see the real me.

My words can reach further than I can ever expect to travel. Far beyond the land and sky, or any distance between you and I.

My words can make you happy, whenever you're feeling down. They can guide you through the darkness when the sun goes down.

Like the moon, they can guide the way. As you continue on your way.

My words are kind and sincere and true. I can use them to tell you every little thing about you.

I won't sugar coat, or insist we're in the same boat. You can choose to listen or ignore; I'll tell you again like I have once before.

I choose to remain in the shadows, to tell my story that nobody knows.

I would lend you a candle, for a light you can handle. As like I said my inner light doesn't shine so bright.

Use the candle and stay close to me to hear all my words that I have to say. About all the things I've seen along the way.

My words can take you on a journey of twists and turns, highs and lows. Through a land of wonder nobody else knows.

I can use them to paint a picture so you can see, all the beautiful things that are surrounding me.

From the birds in the trees to the animals on the ground. There is so much to see, if you stop and look around.

There is truly beauty in this vast land. Come with me and I'll show you around.

The animals and places, there is so much to see. I can never get bored of using my words to help you see visually.

The time has come for me to come out from the shadows. So, people can put a face to the author of words that they know.

My inner light is shining brighter, as my journey continues through the night into the day where it is lighter.

You can see for yourself, all that I have told you about. From the birds in the trees to the animals on the ground.

You can see the true beauty of this vast land. No longer need to guide you or show you around.

I'll still use my words each and every day, because they bring happiness and sunshine with every word I say.

PLANTED NOT BURIED

Life threw me to the sands
Buried me in the darkness of the earth.
I was trampled on, given up on since birth.
Grief had me in her mercy
Life laughed at my misery

They mocked "She'll never come out from it"
My soul cried out "Its hurts being here"
Little did they know I was a seed
Planted not buried

Though I might be surrounded by darkness
But the light in me will be kindled alight
And shine through this darkness
I will establish my roots in the sands
And shoot my stems, pull out my branches
I will stand tall, planted firm
And be in the light again.

ROBYN

Robyn, you have been caged for far too long.
It's time for you to be released and sing your fight song.
Let your spirit sore high,
high up into the sky.
Learn from your life,
try and move forward without further strife.
Birds can only fly forward, so as in your name's sake,
That is a decision only you can make.

Look to your future, let it shine bright.
Like a star shining in the sky at night.
Spread your wings and don't settle, be like a bird that migrates.
To a bigger and brighter land, a new life in the United States.
The chance is yours, so grab it with both hands.
How far you go depends,
on you standing tall and holding your head high.
Looking on up and forward up into the sky.
Robyn once you are free from your cage,
It's time to start writing a new story, page by page.

A new story, with a beginning, middle and eventually an end.
I'll be there like the Northern Star To guide you.
For anytime you get lost and forget what to do.
I'm not just your mother but a friend.
But on me, you will no longer have only just to depend.
Just know, wherever you go and whatever you do.
You have a whole new family and world waiting for you.
Picking up and starting anew, only looking back behind you.

To realize how far you have come and to see the mountain of life that you have overcome.

So, my beautiful Robyn, start preparing for your cage door to be opened.

And your new story to be penned.

As for me, well I'll say for every Robin I see.

I will know you're out there living a life so worthy.

REMEMBER US

What did Jesus have in common with us men and women who fought in the wars?

The answer is, we all sacrificed ourselves. So that you could have a better, safer future. Jesus bore the cross and died for all of our sins, as us men and women fought for peace and safer world. So, all of our children and our children's children could live. Our lives were our gifts to give.

God had his own way of ridding the world of famine, greed, sin and treacherous people. But here we are in 2023, just as cold and greedy. We as an entire world live in it, always wanting more. More land, more weapons and resources anything that would bring a profit.

Remember Us men and women who gave our lives for the cause. So today please pray and celebrate in Remembrance for us all. Not just the ones who have died but also for the ones still fighting. Who can say they did their best and tried.

Wherever there is conflict and destruction, let there be peace, forgiveness and kindness to all. Allow us time to heal as entire Nations all throughout the world.

The Great British soldier did not grow old. Instead, our spirits ascended, whilst our bodies laid out in the cold. The flame still shines with light in our eyes. Our bodies rest, while the flag forever flies.

In the green and gold fields across the horizon, where battles were fought and lost my men and women. We today fly flags for their yesterday's and for our tomorrow. We live on with pain and sorrow.

Our oceans and seas and blood red streams, are now our graveyard of peaceful dreams. Above the sunburnt plain, whether night and day, we see rainbows after the rain. Remember Us, Remember our pain.

We did what needed to be done, to develop a life and world worth living. For every father's daughter or a mother's son each battle was fought and won. We fought in honor for your freedom. Remember Us all each and every man and women, those that have gone and those yet to come.

Remember Us the Great British soldiers, our light burns on. Not just for those that died but those who grew older and still to come. When the nights were cold and dark and danger lurks, we fought with swords and guns, whatever works.

Forget Us not, remember Us must, for our sacrifice. For the strength and pain, we had to endeavor. Our lights have gone but our flame lasts forever. Remember Us as we have gone, the world we leave where it rightfully should belong. To the young and old and brave and strong.

In the face of any challenge, remember Us. We died and raised to God above and strive to leave the world with peace and love. Remember Us, we fought for you to have the opportunity to live and learn. We did not waiver when it came to our turn. The paths we trod showed our courage and commitment witnessed by God. Just as Jesus died for us. We did our best. So please remember us as we lay and rest.

RESOLUTIONS

There is a new dawn, there is a new day. I'm out here trying to find a way.

A way to work on my inhibitions, finding a new me from the old one you once knew.

There is no path I won't follow to realize my New Year Resolutions.

Let my past remain where it is, for it is my future where my heart is. A future with new Expectations, Ambitions and Resolutions.

There is a change coming on this road to discovery. An uphill journey to finding a new me but I know I'll find a way to work on my inhibitions. For there is no path I won't follow to help realize my New Year's Resolutions.

It's a new me it's a new you, share the love for all to view. Let it be seen from miles away, the past is the past and shall remain that way.

The path I'm on, is where the road lies. For the person who is before you truly try. Let no one stop them on their road, their journey of self-discovery.

An uphill journey to finding a new me. I know I'll find a way to work on my inhibitions, for there is no path I won't follow to realize my New Year's Resolutions.

Robyn Leigh Butera Deakin

THE STORY OF MY LIFE

It's weird how my life has turned out.
How my mother was neither here or there.
How she was absent my whole life,
How life with her was like the edge of a knife.
But now that she has passed. I remember
How she was always more concerned with men around her.
Consumed with luster of a new guy,
of the month nothing ever lasting, I wondered why?
Rather than retrieving our clothes from off the line.

How she was never a stable mother.
I was small and delicate and she neglected me and my older brother.
I suppose I got to see more of the real her as I got older.
Until eventually she became bitter and her mood became colder.
It's weird how I didn't think this would ever be my life
How I went down the darkened path myself
How I followed her unintentionally,
becoming consumed by men and drinking so evidently.
How I became pregnant at 18 and a mum at 19.

How I failed to see the wrong turn and
how I lost myself, not knowing that men were so mean.
It's weird how I never wanted to be like my mother
How when I became a mother I changed
How when I became a mother, I felt incomplete
Feeling the need to be swept off my feet.
I hate it really, how I have never abandoned my kids

Or mistreated them, but through life's cruel twist and turned
I lost them all, I remember how I cried until my eyes burned.
Now I am older, I'm aware of my mistakes.
I will rebuild, however long it takes.
My children may not be by my side,
But I know where they are.
Only a stone's throw away, not very far.

They are older too and have made me a proud mum.
I don't know what I'd do or how I'd live without them.
This is the story of my life; it has gone around in a full circle.
I've been through a lot, enough to write a journal.
About having loved and lost, my kids are my life, my love is eternal.
If you ever think you know my story, The Story of My Life....

You don't so take a seat, pull up a pew,
I'll start from the moment I became a wife.
You may need a tissue, 1 or 2 should do.
When you have finished it, right to the end,
Come and have a drink with me my one and only true friend.

TIME

Time is all but an essence. Slipping through our hands.
It has no pretense; it flows freely making no demands.
Whether it be seconds, minutes, hours, or days.
Time can be spent in many ways.
It may go quick or it may go slow.

It is more than a pendulum swinging to and for.
Time spent with loved ones is the best.
It stands alone, longer than any test.
Spend it wisely, never in haste.
Don't let a single second go to waste.
If I could turn back the hands of time.
I'd go as far as I can, to a point I could make you mine.
All the time we could have had.

We could have always been happy and never sad.
Some people have too much time,
Whereas some don't have enough.
When managing your time,
Try and balance the smooth with the rough.
Spend it with family and friends.
Embracing and engaging until the very end.
Time is precious, something to value.
Time is all about discovering me and you.

WELL WISHES

I hope your OK, sleeping well and getting plenty of rest.
So, you can continue doing your best.
Time after time,
You may fall out of line.
But you always bounce back,
You have a knack of getting back on track.

Go follow your dream,
Moving forward, not looking where you have been.
No time for feeling blue,
Not when you have your whole future ahead of you.
Go and showcase the best of you.
Is all that I want you to do.
Step aside and reach up far,
Like the shining star that you are.

Go shine your light so bright,
Go shine on all through the night.
You are the most vibrant star in sight.
Take comfort in knowing and try not despair,
I may be in body here but I'm always in spirit there.

WHY?

Why now, when I'm not in a position to do anything?
Why do you make my heart skip a beat and flutter and sing?
Why are you so under my skin?
Why are you stirring sensations within?
Why are you so kind and make me feel appreciated, not at all how I anticipated?
Why after only a short amount of time?
Do I feel like I know you so well, as if we were together in a previous lifetime?
Why does it feel so much like heaven? I'm glad it's not hell!

Why are you always on my mind?
Oh, how I wish you could be mine.
Why is our friendship so important to me?
Why are you probably the only person to actually get me?
I want to get to know you for the rest of eternity.
So, can you answer, why you're under my skin or stirring sensations within?
Why is knowing you like being in heaven?

You by far stand out and are the best among all men.
I pray to God for that and say Amen.
Why are all these thoughts and feelings flowing through my head?
Is this what is preventing me from sleep while in bed.
Why can't I sleep and meet you in my dream?
Why is life so mean?
I ask you and I, why oh why oh why?

WHEN I WAS YOUNG

When I was young
I could run really fast
I'd race the sun all day
At night sleep on the grass
I'd lay under the stars
Just watch them shine
A smile on my face
Nothing on my mind

These days I wish
I could run that fast
First place I'd run
Is straight to the past

I'd blow through the years
Just like the wind
Come in for a landing
Do it all over again
I want to feel
How I felt back then

The world was beautiful
Everyone was my friend
I want to run free
I want to run wild
I want to see the world
Through the eyes of a child

A GIFT OF LOVE

She was more beautiful than nature,
Her soul radiated beyond compare;
But she was nothing without his vapor,
Nourishing the roots of her despair.

Without him, she was just a flower,
Withering away from her existence,
Needing him to give her a shower
So, her beauty could go the distance.

He knew without her, tides would change
And he would just be washed out to sea,
So, he made sure to stay within her range
By holding onto her so gracefully.

The more he held on the greater they grew
And loves true beauty started to transcend
That was then, both their souls knew
They'd become more than just a friend.

Without each other, life wouldn't exist
As there would be no love to ever share
So, they embraced one another and kissed,
Showing just how much, they truly care.

"ABOUT ME? ABOUT YOU?"

Songs I write, and poems I pen,
And all the stories, they contain within,
Are they true to my life? Do you want to know?
Well, They're probably not ....but maybe so.

My words are inspired by world events,
Just old stories, all past tense.
Songs about life, in a familiar key,
But it doesn't mean...... they're all about me.

My writings may include, family and friends,
Or relationships coming to bitter ends.
Silly things that some people do,
Hell, my poems could even...... be about you.

So, I'll bring this story to a gentle close,
Who, I write about, no one knows.
I never really know how a poem may go,
But when I figure them out ....I'll let you know.

DANCE IN THE RAIN

Don't wait for the storm to pass, learn to dance in the rain.
Those sweet falling raindrops, will never put out your flame

Spinning around in circles, with your face to the sky
Is one of life's simple pleasures, that no money can buy

If the night is a mystery, don't wait for the sun to rise
You can still find your way, with the moonlight in your eyes

A warm southern breeze, gently guiding you along
A woodpecker keeping rhythm, knocking out a song

After a bolt of lightning, you're going to feel the thunder
Instead of being afraid, take a minute and wonder

What does it mean, when it comes down from above
How does it feel, to be floating on the wings of love.

It's a night to remember, with static in the air
The world at a distance and wind in your hair

You'll always taste the sweetness, of the rain on your tongue
Long after you've forgotten, what it means to be young

MARIA APARECIDA GUIMARAES (*CIDA GUIMARAES*)

COUNTRY: BRAZIL

ABOUT ME

Cida Guimarães, short for Maria Aparecida Guimarães.

Brazilian, a widow, mother of three children, and two granddaughters. A lover of nature, reading, arts, people, knowledge and travelling. Considers writing vital to get in touch with her feelings and deal with them. So, by reading her writings, you'll get to know part of her.

THE REASONS I WRITE POEMS:

"I write poetry to let my soul speak. It's kind of a call to put out all that is going on inside of me.

MY MESSAGE TO THE WORLD:

I believe the world needs more empathy, love, and unrestricted acceptance of people's diversity of creed, race and political orientation; less greed, criticism, prejudice, and preconceived ideas. The humanity also needs to develop their sense of respect for one another, the climate and the surroundings to achieve and maintain **PEACE** with ourself, the others and the world at large.

If people of all nations make an effort to understand one another, without trying to make them think and behave like they do, there won't be so many conflicts and wars.

Cida Guimarães

CHAPTER FOUR
MARIA APARECIDA GUIMARAES
(*CIDA GUIMARAES*)

MURALHAS

Que triste quando tudo que desejamos é o bem do outro
e somos rejeitados, mal interpretados.
Como transpor muros de negação, muralhas de proteção?

É mais fácil aceitar o incrível, o fantasmagórico, terrível do que crer no crível e simplório. Mudar é sofrido, difícil. Precisamos questionar nossas crenças, despir nossas sofrências. Olhar para o novo com confiança, que uma mudança trará bonança.

Só com muito amor e crença que a força deste sentimento possa derrubar a espessa muralha de desentendimentos e construir pontes de confiança.

WALLS

How sad when all we want is the good of others
and we are rejected, misunderstood.
How to overcome walls of denial, walls of protections?

It is easier to accept the incredible, the ghostly, the terrible than to believe the believable and simplistic. Changing is painful, difficult. We need to question our beliefs, reveal our sufferings.

Look at the new with confidence that a change will bring prosperity.
Only with a lot of love and belief can the strength of this feeling be able to break down the thick wall of disagreements, and build bridges of trust.

ESPERANÇA

Minutos de aflição. Dor, desespero, maldição!
É a vida a nos testar. A confiança é pequena, a coragem enferma.

São muitos problemas esgotando nossos esquemas minando
nossas defesas.
E, de repente, tudo começa a mudar e o mundo,
recomeça a brilhar.

É a esperança iluminando nossas crenças, apagando a descrença,
nos auxiliando, novamente, a sorrir e a nossa vida seguir,

Com a coragem dada pela fé e muita esperança, sempre,
para enfrentar
novos dias de fel, na certeza que, logo, novamente,
virão os de mel.

HOPE

Minutes of distress: Pain, despair, curse!
It´s life testing us. Trust is small, courage is weak.

There are many problems exhausting our schemes
Mining our defenses. And suddenly, everything starts
to change, and the world begins to shine again.

It´s hope illuminating our beliefs, erasing disbelief,
helping us, again, to smile and go on with our lives.

With the courage given by Faith, and always with a lot of hope
to face new days of bile in certainty that,
soon, honey days will come again.

QUE MUNDO É ESTE?

Mundo de faz de conta, de pouca ternura, muita hipocrisia,
e falso apreço.
Mundo de palavras vazias, verdades veladas, distorcidas,
Mundo de omissões, de abismos nas interações. Mundo de
artifícios, lacunas, meias palavras, do não elogio e aplauso quando
gostamos ou apupo quando odiamos, erguendo muros de
proteção, barreiras na comunicação.

Que lindo e ideal seria este mundo se fossemos verdadeiros,
abrindo nossos corações, expressando reais emoções numa onda
de respeito, amor e calor.

WHAT WORLD IS THIS?

World of make believe, of little tenderness,
a lot of hypocrisy, and false appreciation.
World of empty words, veiled, distorted truths.

World of omissions, of abysses in interactions.
World of artifices, gaps, half words, of not praising
and applauding when we like it, or jeering when we hate it,
erecting protective barriers in communication.

How beautiful and ideal this world would be
if we were true, opening our hearts,
expressing real emotions in a wave of respect,
love and warmth!

CAMINHANDO

Caminhando ou correndo, passeando ou atropelando,
surfando ou se afogando, vamos pela vida usufruindo ou
usurpando, construindo ou destruindo, rindo ou chorando,
agradecendo ou praguejando.

Vamos observando os caminhos, escolhendo e apreciando as
rotas? Curtindo os acertos, mas atentos aos percalços para não
sucumbir nas crateras? Ou seguimos vendados, desatentos,
incautos e ingratos na espera de mudanças?

Nossa caminhada pode ser linda e plena de fantasia
se curtirmos a beleza de cada novo dia.
É, entretanto, necessária a certeza que tudo depende de nosso
olhar cuidadoso para que nossa jornada seja segura,
repleta de atenção, amor e alegria.

WALKING

Walking or jogging. strolling or running over
Surfing or drowning, we go through life
Enjoying or usurping, laughing or crying
Thanking or swearing.

Do we observe the paths choosing and enjoying the routes,
the successes, but paying attention to the pitfalls
so as not to succumb in the craters?
Or do we remain blindfolded, inattentive, incautious
and ungrateful, waiting for changes?

Our journey can be beautiful and full of fantasy
if we enjoy the beauty of each new day.
However, it is necessary to be sure that everything
depends on our careful attention so that
our journey is safe, full of love and joy.

GUERRA E PAZ

Fronteira entre pensamentos divergentes de ideias, crenças, leis,
culturas, políticas, atos e territórios de outros países.

Difícil respeitar o direito de ser e pensar diferente, de defender
fronteiras e criar barreiras se a cobiça for prevalente.

Enquanto não reconhecermos que somos indivíduos únicos,
e diversos será difícil conviver em paz e harmonia.

Há que respeitar os limites e autonomia dos outros povos
para garantir que os nossos sejam observados.
Tudo começa no indivíduo e se espalha para o coletivo.
Só com respeito, sem egoísmo a paz irá prevalecer e a sociedade
sobreviver.

Bombas estourando, sonhos se esfacelando.
Multidões buscando abrigo.
Destruição e caos se instalando em mais uma guerra.
A paz será sempre uma utopia se a cobiça prevalecer.

Paz entre irmãos, cidadãos, países, continentes se desfaz, vira
quimera
A guerra como uma peste que se propaga apaga o bom e belo
Espalhando a praga do desentendimento, trazendo o horror do
inferno.

Enterra sonhos, matando e deformando. Que os homens possam
buscar entendimento e conciliação. Que o mundo veja a
transformação da ambição em pacificação.

WAR AND PEACE

Boundaries among divergent thoughts, ideas, beliefs, laws,
cultures, policies, acts, and territories of other countries as
it is difficult to respect the right to be and think differently,
to defend borders and create barriers if greed is prevalent.

As long as we do not recognize that we are unique and diverse
individuals, it will be difficult to live together in peace and
harmony
The limits and autonomy of other peoples must be respected to
ensure that ours are observed.
It all starts with the individual and spreads to the collective.
Only with respect, without selfishness, will peace prevail and
society will survive.

Bombs exploding, dreams crumbling.
Crowds seeking shelter.
Destruction and chaos ensuing in yet another war.
Peace will always be a utopia if greed prevails.

Peace between brothers and sisters, citizens, countries, continents
are unraveling, becoming a chimera.
War, like a spreading plague, erases the good and beautiful,
spreading the chaos of misunderstanding,
bringing the horror of hell.
It buries dreams, kills and deforms. May men seek understanding
and conciliation. May the world see the transformation of
ambition in peacemaking.

SOMBRAS

Tudo são sombras: de um olhar, de um amor, uma flor, uma dor, Sombras de mim, do que fui, do que vivi, do que sonhei, do que perdi. Retratos mal definidos de sentidos e histórias vividas e resolvidas, perdidas, dentro de mim.

Negativos e borrões não revelados, indistintos,
desnudando os escombros e transmutando meus medos
em esperança e crença de força e novos anseios

SHADOWS

All are shadows: of a look, a love, a flower, a pain,
Shadows of me, of what I was, what I lived,
what I dreamed, what I lost.
Ill-defined portrayals of meanings and stories lived and resolved,
lost, within us.

Undeveloped, indistinct negatives and smudges.
Shadow, let the light illuminate my meanders,
Barring the rubble and transmuting my fears
in hope and belief of strength and new longings.

PRECE

Esperança que aquece o coração, abastece a fé, faz nossas orações ecoarem e traz a certeza que a fase difícil vai passar, e dias melhores hão de chegar.

Amor, coragem, e determinação para visualizar alternativas, e soluções de conforto, que amenizem a dor do corpo e da alma, renovem a saúde, e tragam dias de calmaria.

Oh pai de misericórdia! Escuta nossa prece e nos brinda com sua clemência, amainando a dor e fazendo o milagre da cura acontecer.

PRAYER

Hope that warms the heart, fuels faith, makes our prayers echo and brings the certainty that the difficult phase will pass, and better days will come.

Love, courage, and determination to visualize alternatives, and comfort solutions, that ease the pain of body and soul, renew health, and bring days of calm.

O Father of Mercy! He hears our prayer and offers us his mercy, easing the pain and making the miracle of healing happen.

VOLTAR

Voltar para quem, para o quê, para onde?
Voltar a sermos quem fomos, reviver nossa história,
fazendo, talvez, opções distintas, reescrevendo partes dela?

Voltar é, sempre, recomeçar. Nada será igual. Nem nós mesmos. Faríamos diferente? Será? Sonhamos, às vezes, em viver este filme de ficção, "Retorno ao passado" em que é possível voltar a lugares, reaver pessoas queridas, revisitar momentos e situações especiais.
Nesta aventura, tudo é perfeito!

Será que se voltássemos seríamos iguais? E a realidade circundante, como seria? Provavelmente distinta. Nada permanece inalterado, nem mesmo nossa emoção.

A melhor opção é ficar no hoje, e buscar viver cada segundo, da melhor maneira possível como se não fosse haver um amanhã de forma que não queiramos voltar.

Será possível? Vale tentar!

GOING BACK!

Back to whom, to what, to where?
Go back to who we were, to relive our history,
making, perhaps, different choices, rewriting parts of it?

To return is always to start over.
Nothing will ever be the same. Neither will ourselves be.
Would we do it differently? Is it possible? We dream, sometimes, of living this fictional film, "Return to the Past" in which it is possible to return to places, revisit loved ones, special moments and situations. In this adventure, everything is perfect!

Would we be the same if we would go back? And what about the surrounding reality, what would it be like? Probably distinct. Nothing remains unchanged, not even our emotion. The best option is to stay in today, and try to live every second, in the best possible way as if there´s not going to be a tomorrow so that we won´t desire to go back. Is it possible? It's worth a try!

MILAGRES

Tantos, alguns tão pequenos, múltiplos, que não os notamos ou valorizamos: a noite, o ocaso com suas trevas, e merecido descanso, o nascer do sol, a iluminação, a labuta, vida que recomeça.

As estações e suas intempéries; cada uma com seu propósito, suas dádivas e pragas. O bom e o mau, as alegrias e as tristezas, surpresas e decepções, ganhos e perdas.

É, sempre, a vida e seus milagres de constante renovação de nossas oportunidades. Ciclos que começam e terminam. Etapas de vida, de sentimentos, interesses que se concluem, esgotam e mudam.

Movimento de eterna renovação. Cada momento, cada encruzilhada, cada escolha é o milagre da vida nos dando a chance de ser e fazer diferente, de sermos outros, e ainda assim, nós mesmos.

MIRACLES

So many, some so small, multiple, that we don't notice or value them: the night, the sunset with its darkness, and well-deserved rest, the sunrise, the illumination, the toil, life that begins again.

The seasons and their inclement weather; each with its own purpose, its gifts and plagues. The good and the bad, the joys and the sorrows, surprises and disappointments, gains and losses.

It is, always, life and its miracles of constant renewal, of our opportunities. Cycles that begin and end. Stages of life, of feelings, interests that are concluded, exhausted and change.

Movement of eternal renewal. Every moment, every crossroads, every choice is the miracle of life giving us the chance to be and do differently, to be others,
and yet, ourselves.

AS CURVAS DO CAMINHO

Expectativas frustradas, planejamentos destruídos,
Esperança abalada. Insegurança!
Sempre a vida te surpreendendo com suas curvas inesperadas.

Há que acreditar e lutar sabendo que só podemos mudar a nós mesmo, desenvolver paciência e resiliência para aceitar o que não dá para alterar.

Hercúlea a tarefa de abrir caminho entre pedras e espinhos, que te ferem, alteram, mas te ajudam a crescer, talvez, quem sabe, florescer.

THE CURVES OF THE PATH

Frustrated expectations, destroyed plans,
Hope shaken. Insecurity!
Always life surprising you with its unexpected curves.

We have to believe and fight knowing that we can only change ourselves, develop patience and resilience to accept what cannot be changed.

Herculean is the task of making our way through stones and thorns, which wound you, alter you, but help you to grow, perhaps, who knows, also flourish.

É PRECISO ACREDITAR

Quando estás perdido, tudo sem sentido, de pernas por ar
não tens mais o que dar; estás oco, morto por dentro.
Precisas que nem louco de esperança, de luz, de fé
que pouco a pouco a vida vai seguir e serás mais feliz.

Há que lembrar que tudo é passageiro, e vai passar,
a luz voltará a brilhar,
A paz e a saúde a imperar.
É preciso acreditar.

YOU HAVE TO BELIEVE

When you are lost, meaningless,
upside down, having nothing left to give,
hollow, dead inside, you need like crazy hope,
faith and light that little by little
life will go on and you will be happier.

We have to remember that everything is fleeting,
and it will pass, the light will shine again,
Peace and health will prevail.
You have to believe.

SER INTEIRO

Turbilhão de pensamentos, sentimentos, ideias, caos!
Que venha a calmaria, o equilíbrio entre a razão e a emoção,
a sensação de estar pleno, a placidez!

Ter a alma em paz na entrega do melhor de si,
sem nada a esperar, só amor a entregar.
Alma, corpo, espírito em harmonia, integrados
Na beleza de um ser inteiro,

Somos, quase sempre, divididos, razão e coração
entre sentimentos, decisões. Precisamos ouvir nossa voz
interior para encontrar nosso caminho e ser, estar inteiros,
Sermos UM.

BE WHOLE

Whirlwind of thoughts, feelings, ideas, chaos!
May the calm come, the balance between reason and emotion,
the feeling of being full, the placidity!

To have the soul at peace in the delivery of the best of oneself,
With nothing to hope for, only love to give.
Soul, body, spirit in harmony, integrated
in the beauty of a whole being,

We are almost always divided, reason and heart
between feelings, decisions. We need to hear our inner voice
to find our way and to be whole,

MAR DA VIDA

E a vida vem em ondas, como o mar, me puxando,
derrubando, revigorando, mas também me afogando,
E eu vou me esquivando, deleitando, refrescando,
apavorando, surfando, mas também surtando.

Mil sensações, colorações, trepidações, enchendo
nossos corações de múltiplas sensações, infinitas emoções.

SEA OF LIFE

And life comes in waves, like the sea, pulling me,
knocking me down, invigorating, but also drowning me,
And I'm dodging, delighting, refreshing,
Freaking out, surfing, but also cracking.

A thousand colors, sensations, trepidations, filling
our hearts with multiple sensations, endless emotions.

CÉU E INFERNO

Tudo muda a cada instante. É a vida acontecendo. Não há como congelar ou anular. Há que viver, aprender, reter ou esquecer; é a vida acontecendo, te chacoalhando e ensinando. São lições, por vezes, dolorosas, difíceis, necessárias; outras passam despercebidas para voltarem a acontecer, te fazendo reviver emoções para finalmente aprender.
Será?

Aprender para sair do inferno.
Céu e inferno se alternam e vamos da alegria ao pranto, do entusiasmo ao desespero. Tudo vivido, questionado, sofrido, revivido para que pouco a pouco possamos florescer, e melhorar para viver o céu.

HEAVEN AND HELL

Everything changes at every second. It's life happening. There is no way to freeze or void. We must live, learn, retain or forget; Its life going on, shaking us, teaching us. Some are, sometimes, painful, difficult, necessary lessons; Others go unnoticed to happen again, making you relive emotions, and finally learn.
Will you?

Learn your way out of hell.
Heaven and hell alternate and we go from joy to tears, from enthusiasm to despair. Everything lived, questioned, suffered, relived so that little by little we can flourish, and improve to live heaven.

ENCANTAMENTO

O amanhecer na praia com sua miríade de cores, nuances;
os morros envolvidos numa bruma, o sol querendo despontar,
criando reflexos prateados no mar, que vai rebentando na areia
com sua espuma branca.
Puro encantamento!

Uma sensação mágica de paz, prazer, envolvimento como se Deus estivesse nos abraçando, nos protegendo, nos mostrando tudo que temos, a beleza que nos circunda, e que todo o resto não importa.

É preciso deixar nossa necessidade de controle, de sofrer por antecipação, colocar tudo nas mãos de nosso pai e viver a beleza de cada momento único. Deixar que a magia e beleza de sua criação nos envolva e fortaleça.

ENCHANTMENT

The sunrise on the beach with its myriad of colors, nuances;
The hills shrouded in mist, the sun wanting to rise, creating silver reflections in the sea, which bursts on the sand with its white foam.
Pure enchantment!

A magical feeling of peace, pleasure, involvement as if God is embracing us, protecting us, showing us everything we have, the beauty that surrounds us, and that everything else doesn't matter.

It is necessary to let go of our need for control, to suffer in anticipation, to put everything in our father's hands and live the beauty of each unique moment. Let the magic and beauty of his creation envelop and strengthen us.

SORRIA!!

Sensação linda a de nos sentirmos vistos, reconhecidos, apreciados naquilo que realmente somos, e que nem sempre demonstramos.

É uma alegria que inunda, e suaviza as dores sentidas e vertidas.
Uma sensação de plenitude, este espetáculo de renovação da vida:
Um novo dia, sorria!

SMILE

It's a beautiful feeling to feel seen, recognized, appreciated for what we really are, and what we don't always show. It is a joy that floods, and softens the pain felt and shed.
A feeling of fullness, a spectacle of life renewal.
A new day, smile!

SERES CONTROVERSOS

Como somos contraditórios!
Infelizes na felicidade,
sofrendo, mas amando,
querendo o impossível, mas
brigando com o possível.

Eternos insatisfeitos,
buscamos, nem sabemos o quê;
a realidade é sempre frustrante,
aquém de nossas expectativas,
que são, quase sempre, irreais.

Queremos perfeição, mas somos imperfeitos,
buscamos um ideal imaginário, quando temos o real possível,
tentando entender o outro,
quando não nos conhecemos.

Somos dúbios, intrigantes!
Melhor seria se fossemos rio de águas mansas,
plácido e tranquilo, do que mar de águas revoltas,
que tudo engolfa e destrói.

CONTROVERSIAL BEINGS

How contradictory we are!
Unhappy in happiness, suffering,
but loving, wanting the impossible,
but fighting against the possible. Eternally dissatisfied,
we seek, we don't even know what; reality is always frustrating,
below our expectations,

We want perfection, but we're totally imperfect,
Search an imaginary ideal, when we have the possible real,
trying to understand the other when we don't even know
ourselves.

We are dubious, intriguing!
It would be better if we were a river of calm waters,
placid and tranquil, than a sea of raging waters,
that engulfs and destroys everything.

PACIÊNCIA!

É tão dificil só viver o momento presente,
sem ansiedade, sem expectativas!
Como ser paciente, saber esperar, aguardar o desenrolar das situações, sem antecipar problemas, ou criar desfechos?

A vida, vai, sempre, nos surpreender, e quando parecer que não há rotas de fuga,
e a paciência estiver por um fio, inesperadamente, tudo pode mudar, o cenário se alterar, e novas esperanças criar.

É preciso, entretanto, calma, tolerância, e muita confiança para enfrentar, com coragem e muita paciência, as dificuldades do caminho, para no final, talvez,
alcançar um abençoado estado de descanso.

PATIENCE

Patience! It's so difficult to just live in the present moment, without anxiety, without expectations! How to be patient, know how to wait for situations to unfold, without anticipating problems, or creating outcomes?

Life will always surprise us, and when it seems like
there are no escape routes, and patience is hanging by a thread, unexpectedly, everything can change, the scenario and new hopes are created.

However, it requires calm, tolerance, and a lot of confidence
to face, with courage and a lot of patience,
the difficulties along the way, in order to, in the end, perhaps,
reach a blessed state of rest.

VERTENTE!

Por que, tristeza, és como uma vertente, que não para de jorrar?
Nem sei exatamente o quê, porquê, só tento entender, sem poder...

Que seres intricados somos!
Difícil saber o que guia nosso querer
o que acalma nosso viver, e acalenta nosso ser!

Viver implica em sofrer,
mas também em saber escolher
e, aí reside o resolver entre acolher, ceder, contradizer, ou verter...

Nossa alma, como uma fonte
verte sua dor em torrente de lágrimas, que não cessam até
a vertente parar de jorrar.

STREAM!

Why, sadness, you are like a stream that never stops flowing? I
don't even know exactly, why, what for, I just try to understand,
without being able to...
What intricate beings we are! It's hard to know what guides our
desires what calms our living, and warms our being!

Living means suffering, but also knowing how to choose and,
therein lies the decision between accepting, giving in,
contradicting, or spilling...
Our soul, like a fountain pours out its pain in a torrent of tears,
which do not cease until the strand stops gushing.

MULHERES

Filhas, mães, avós, sozinhas, casadas, descasadas, de todas as nacionalidades; brancas, pretas, amarelas, baixas, altas, magras, gordas, bem ou mal amadas, atuantes ou observantes, donas de si ou dependentes, são e dão origem a vida.

São a fonte de poemas, de amores, e dores, de colo, de sustento e alento. Simbolizam o belo e pleno, o supremo e o profano. Dão vida, e se multiplicam na vida. São fonte inesgotável de afeto, e colo, paz e união.

Minha homenagem a todas as mulheres, neste livro, que é delas para elas e eles. Lendo estes poemas irão conhecer mais dos sentimentos e visões das mulheres mundo afora.
Tenho orgulho de ser mulher.

WOMEN

Daughters, mothers, grandmothers, single, married, unmarried, of all nationalities; white, black, yellow, short, tall, thin, fat; well or badly loved, active or observant, self-possessed or dependent, are the source and give rise to life.

They are the inspiration of poems, loves, pains, arms, they provide sustenance and encouragement. They symbolize the beautiful and complete, the supreme and the profane. They give life, and multiply in life. They are an inexhaustible source of affection, and lap, peace and union.

My tribute to all women, I´m proud of being one.

Cida Guimarães

ROSE R. SALES

COUNTRY: PHILIPPINES

WHY DO YOU WRITE POETRY?

When I couldn't find the strength to vocalize every sentiment, poetry was there. When no one was willing to listen to my swarm of thoughts within, poetry was there. When I, alone, was drowned by the cataclysm of emotions; the light was nowhere to be found and I lost my direction, poetry was still there.

No words can delineate how poetry has saved me. Not even one imagery can thoroughly portray what it truly means to me. But here's what I'm certain—poetry is amazingly beautiful and immortal, for it can touch one's heart and dwell in the soul of any individual.

WHAT IS YOUR MESSAGE TO THE WORLD?

Perfection does not exist in this world. But if you dig deeper from the surface, you will realize that everyone possesses beauty and brokenness at the same time—including you. And it's alright, that's the nature of life. So, instead of pointing out your flaws, you must embrace and love yourself even more

BY: ROSE SALES

Pseudonyms: Amaranthine Briar and Akahana

CHAPTER FIVE
ROSE R. SALES

EARTH FAIRY

In the mere point of view
of the foreign of this land,
they would never understand
the roots of my soul.

They would never comprehend
how the vines kissed me
as they intricately wrapped
all around my body,
and it's not nasty but rather pretty.

I adore the downpour
that awakens the breeze
along with the sun's rays
that seep into my skin
which allows me to bloom
despite being from rock bottom.

I am one with the forest,
but unfortunately,
the eyes that had only wandered
within the bounds of the city lights
would never see its beauty.

UNSINKABLE AMBITION

Her skin is adorned with pixie dusts
that makes her stand out
even in times when shadows reign.
She flies like a fairy in light pink,
that even in the midst of monstrous waves,
her passion won't sink.
But every starless night,
there's this heavy thing—
more like a burden inside
that she carries because of the pressure
of the different races in life.
She endures it because she cares.
She wants to succeed, so she can help.

This is the ultimate reason why
this lady is unsinkable:
When she puts her heart
onto something,
she will move heaven and earth
just to make it happen.
Yes, she is ambitious,
but her heart is close to earth,
expect her not to forget
where she came from
despite tasting the air on top.

SILENCE SPEAKS

She possesses a melody
that resonates entirely
in a room with a huge crowd,
all I can hear is her sound.

Her mirror eyes can capture
the different phases of nature.
Every gesture she does
seems to be coated with start dusts.

But this world tends to shatter
astonishing souls like her.
They shut the story of her voice,
treated it as if it's a dreadful noise.

Broken, yet remained still.
She said, "This is just a part of the thrill."
Their shadows didn't stain her heart.
Instead, her pieces turned to art.

She flared brighter than ever.
She flew higher than the tower.
Epically, she landed on the peak
when finally, her silence began to speak.

STAR

I am not chasing
for the spotlight
to point only at me.
I just want a share
of its brightness
along with other
dreamers like me.
It may not be my time yet,
but I shall patiently wait.
For my heart believes
that the reason why
there are multiple billions
of stars in the sky,
is for everyone
to have their own light,
and shine wondrously
without having to steal
someone's luminosity
nor overpower anybody.

A MUSE IN THE GALLERY OF WORDS

She reminds me of a portrait
marked by flawless craftsmanship.
She stands out
despite being surrounded
by other intricate arts.
I am enthralled by how
she elaborately ventilates
the fumes inside her heart.
She allows her mind to dip into
the lines of every poetry
she stumbles onto.

She is endearing as a flower's
ambrosial fragrance.
Her inner light reflects
the quintessence of elegance.
I've lost count of metaphors
to portray her beauty,
for she's a crème de la crème
kind of a lady.
I am more than blessed
to have met her in this stanza
of my prosaic life.
Cause now that she's here,
she gives sense to my rhymes.

DAWN OF RESILIENCE

Behind closed doors,
you'll see a lady
with warm tears gushing
out from her eyes.
Pull off the curtains,
still, you'll find no one else
but a maiden who is
questioning her worth.

But as twilight peeks,
the sun gradually rises,
she adorns her face
with a smile crystal-like.
No one would ever notice
the pretension
all over her gaze;
she wouldn't allow it.

"The sky is citrine bright,
feeling blue won't help me
triumph over this fight",
she evoked her courage.

It's the day for redemption.
There's no time for crying.
Her heart is impaired,
but she will keep trying.

IF I DIE

If I die tomorrow,
I wonder what I will do today.
Will I smell the roses
in our little garden?
Will I read all the books
that are unexplored
in the bookshelf?
Will I cook to my heart's content,
and enjoy a delectable meal
with my loved ones?

If I die tomorrow,
I wonder what I will do today.
Will I make amends
to the ones who betrayed me
and forgive them wholeheartedly?
Will I give every last penny
I have in my pocket
to the needy?
Will I spend my remaining time
on the tip of the cliff
as I stare at the sunset?

If it's only hours left
before I take my last breath,
will I be ready to face death?
I'm not quite certain,
but here's my plan,

so, I won't feel any regret:
I will love more than I have
ever loved before.
It may sound vague,
but truly, it isn't.
For when you love,
you will definitely know
what's the right thing to do.
No more worries and doubts.
I won't hold back.

24 hours left
before I meet my own grave,
and within that ephemeral duration,
I will use my heart to the fullest ...
... one last time.

SEAFARER

Deep like a twilight blue ocean
Mysterious like an uncharted island
Not everyone will understand,
For her soul is a special one.

Waves inside her dauntless mind
A heart that's fierce and unwavering
Rocks and stones on the shoreline
Won't stop her from dreaming.

She has an unfathomable passion
Always sets her eyes on the destination
Even if it appears to be murky
Similar to the abyss in the sea
She'll sail with the guidance from above
Navigated by faith, dedication, and love.

BEYOND THE JUDGEMENT

When people body-shamed her,
they thought that they were able
to trample her confidence.
Little did they know,
she armored herself
with tenderness and acceptance.

She is fully aware of her own physique.
She doesn't need anyone
to tell her what's appropriate or not.
Besides, this world is never contented.
It always points out even
the slightest imperfection.

When you're not curvy,
they make fun of your body.
When you're being sexy
they label you as the "queen of immorality"
When you're skinny,
they call you "anorexic" or "unhealthy".
When you're overweight,
they only see your obesity
but never your soul's beauty.
It's always been "too much" or "not enough".
Will they ever say you're "just right"?
These toxic standards
of this judgmental society are exhausting.
She planted in her mind

that she's done with it.
She won't let their piercing words and stares
to shatter her heart again.
She knows she's never perfect,
but guess what?
She loves herself nevertheless.

VERSES OF RENEWAL

Knight in a full-covered armor
is what her prosaic visage,
little did they know that her soul's crux
is not linear but rather similar to a collage.

An aspiring poetic writer—
her goal is to craft a piece unlike any other
cause for a strong woman like her,
depths and rhymes supply her power.

Terrified of the ravenous gazes,
she chose to lay her weapon down
and wore masks of different faces—
ink spilled and paper torn into pieces.

"Halt! I must shut off my surreal dream!"
She screamed this harangue to the sky so dim.
Feeling helpless, feeling worthless
Eyes' sparks are fading, slowly turning grim.

Right from the start she has her own glow,
but because of life's affliction and woe,
she shot her passion away in speed
like it was a blazing arrow.

Indefinite about when to begin again.
But she must hearken and comprehend
the call and true flair she has within:
she's a poetess in the making.

Newly revitalized heart and soul,
she longs to feel it down to her core.
Far from being entirely recovered,
but she is trying to rise and start over.

Even if not everyone will believe
Her spirit won't surrender until it tastes relief
She opts to continue her odyssey,
with a hope of achieving a glorious victory.

PHASES

May the drops of rain
wash all the lingering pain.
Maintain your vision, stay sane.
For your tears will not go in vain.

As the sun finally peeks
through the cloud,
may its rays unveil the thick shroud.
Dry your drenched cheeks.
It shall brighten the dysphoric weeks.

When the wind softly sings,
may it blow everything
that drains and stings.
Lay down the burden you've been lifting,
and gently spread your wings.

The storms and blue days
are only transitory.
Stand, rise, and move on,
for this dark era will soon turn
into summer season.

THE TWILIGHT POETESS

At dusk, in a moonlit darkness
Cruising through the rain is a poetess
Gliding with her silvery, snow-white dress
Whoever passes, shall sense her sadness.

In solitude, she's her own heroine
Spoken her soul, a touch of bitter-saccharine
Aesthetic silhouette; elegance tattooed on her skin
The cradle of her beauty is planted within.

A lady Mockingjay of an ethereal symphony
Whispering endless melodies of agony
Yearning to finally find the harmony
beneath the placid skies of glee, perennially.

A nighthawk she is—a reserved maiden
Sailing in her thoughts, eyes were sunken
But this lady became dauntless, unshaken
For she learned the art of emotions being written.

A MOMENT OF FREEDOM

I always wanted to be free,
Experiencing an adventure spree.
No more anxiety from the crowd,
Just my tiny steps high and proud.

Gliding, wearing my blue dress,
No one will interfere, nor mess.
Just me doing the things I love,
Hoping to see a snow-white dove.

Oh, how wonderful it would be!
To explore the world and see,
How aesthetic it is and divine,
I will definitely be fine.

I will slowly count,
Until I reach the top of the mount.
Spread my wings and fly,
Lost in a blink of an eye.

CRYSTAL SNOW

Wearing a dress coated in silvery frost
Warmth in her seems to be lost
Frigid aura is what surrounds her
Sit with her, and you'll feel like it's winter.

This lady is often found gliding alone
Seldomly speaks, voice in low tone
But this point of view is only one-sided,
For there's a story behind that's left unread.

Books, music, and nature are her peers
Always there to gently wipe her tears
She may appear to be as cold as ice
But stare, you'll see the mist in her eyes.

Her soul's core is not as sharp as a knife
She just prefers to live a solitary life
Her heart isn't as dark and hard as a stone.
She's brilliant like a crystal and soft as a snow.

HIRAETH

Every early morning,
until every late night,
this world keeps on spinning—
I am slowly losing my sight.

I can't keep up with its pace,
I am being dragged away.
One emotion broke the case.
Now, I've gone astray.

This prickling sensation of hiraeth,
devoured my lonely heart.
From left, I'll redirect to the right,
for it's been years since we're apart.

Homesickness knocked on my door.
It's telling me to come home.
You're standing patiently by the shore.
Wait for me, as I finish writing this poem.

There's no turning back from here.
I'll make a U-turn to you, my dear.
I'm coming back because I felt the nostalgia.
Only with you, I shall find my euphoria.
But I'm too late ...

MORNING FLOWER

Sunny springtime blooms reminded me of this lady
Two different flowers that combined in harmony
Has a rosette of small, white petals around a yellow center
Curious? It's a beautiful daisy painted with wonders.

Composite flowers bearing sentimental meanings
Joy, innocence, and new beginnings
This maiden personifies them perfectly
She isn't afraid to take risks despite her purity.

When she cascades her heart's ink on a paper
Poetic fragrance comes out naturally from her
She kept her roots in the soil of writing
Amidst the storms, her stem remained standing.

ONE LAST MEMORY

Ten. We were so close back then.
Almost all of my free time was spent with you,
and you did the same thing too.

Nine. You looked so fine.
Every time I gaze at you, I see this familiar face;
a light expression, I thought it'll never be effaced.

Eight. I believed you were my soulmate.
We automatically complement each other—
when we're together, things turn out better.

Seven. You're such an angel from heaven.
I am a wrecked ship, sunken into the darkness,
yet you didn't waver to dive and fixed my brokenness.

Six. We became victims of fate's tricks.
When I reached out my hand to trace your hair,
tears gushed suddenly cause you're no longer there.

Five. How can I still survive?
My heart unceasingly weeps for your absence.
Every day without you makes no sense.

Four. I am not the same as I was before.
My dearest comrade never came back.
Stuck in isolation, I am losing my track.
Three. I'm afraid there's no remedy.
The pain is insufferable, there's seems to be no cure.

I see you when I close my eyes, what a torture!

Two. I'm almost 22, there's still no "you".
Why did our paths have to intertwine
if we couldn't even stick for an entire lifetime?

One. You are gone.
Cruel world—your story soon ended in tragedy.
Well, so as mine, because I have to live with our one last memory.

Every sunset reminds me of you,
it brings our one last memory back to reality,
like you're sitting here with me too.
As I count down from ten to one
along with the gradient setting sun,
I'll bid my farewell
to the most beautiful heartbreak
I have ever felt—
you.

LYRID METEOR SHOWER

Late nightfall, I sat under the tree's shadow
Reminiscing the day, we met at the meadow
Your radiance sprinkled an enchantment
That was years ago, but I can't forget that moment.

Where are you now, my beloved star?
Month of April—that's written in my memoir
Been here for hours yet you're nowhere to be found
We promised to collide tonight, but you're not around.

Perhaps, our story is meant to be tragic
Our first kiss was only an ephemeral magic
The Lyrid meteor shower finally painted the sky
Along with the tear that flowed from my eye.

I guess, I should start saying 'goodbye'
Thank you for once carving my face with a smile
If in this lifetime the Universe will not favor our love,
"I hope it will in the next", I prayed to God above.

"The Lyrid meteor shower has already passed,
but my love for you will forever last."

WHEN A WRITER WONDERS

I wonder ...

I wonder how would you cherish a poem that was
dedicated to you?

When a person you love gifts you a t-shirt, you wear it often,
don't you?

When a person you love gives you a bouquet of flowers, you smell
it, keep it, and watch over it until it withers, don't you?

When a person you love treats you with food, you eat it with so
much joy and appetite, don't you?

And if I will write you a poem, will you read it from time to time
and treasure it forever, won't you?

But I just thought, I am a mere a stranger who dedicated a poem
to you, I can't expect that you will appreciate it as much as how
you appreciate a written piece when you're loved one
gave it to you.

... saddening but true.

EMERGENCE FROM THE STORM

It was harder than I thought.

I was drowning, barely surviving. The rainstorm has gotten worse every day and it kept on submerging me, dragging my spirit to the deepest hollows.

I was gasping for air. I almost gave up trying to ascend from that excruciating state because I was growing weaker as the time goes by. But when I thought that my world has completely fallen apart, the dark clouds spread wide open to give way for the sunbeams to reach the decaying little flower of hope inside my heart. The light thawed my ice-cold soul, it enriched my shrinking valor, now I transformed into a better person than I was before.

The numbing gray hours of my yesterday were there to mold my entire being; everything was necessary to make me stronger—much bolder to confront whatever adversity lies in my future.

COMFORT EBZAN JAPHETH

COUNTRY: NIGERIA

WHY DO I WRITE POETRY?

I write Poetry as a form of self-expression, to communicate my personal experiences, ideas, and emotions that may be too complex or intimate to share through everyday language. Also, I write Poetry as a means of exploring the nuances of life, allowing me to condense oceans of feeling into a droplet of verse.

WHAT IS YOU MESSAGE TO THE WORLD?

Being a single mother at a very tender age can be challenging, but it can also be an opportunity to grow and learn. You are strong, resilient, and capable of overcoming any obstacle that comes your way. You are not alone, and there are many resources available to help you navigate this journey. Keep pushing forward, and never give up on your dreams. You got this!

CHAPTER SIX
COMFORT EBZAN JAPHETH

TENDER BUD BECOMING A FLOWER

Once a tender bud, now she's a flower so strong,
A lady who faced challenges head-on, all along.
She bloomed amidst chaos, her spirit did grow,
A young mother who refused to let her hardships show.

THE UNSEEN STRENGTH

She faced a journey that was far from fair,
Pregnant at an age when most still unaware.
But within her, strength burned like a fire,
A resolve to rise above, to never tire.

SHATTERED TO HOPE

From innocence shattered, a phoenix emerged,
A young lady whose resilience surged.
She navigated stormy seas with grace,
A testament to the challenges she could embrace.

TRIBULATIONS OF A TEENAGE MOTHER

Through trials and tribulations, she treaded the path,
A teenage mother who knew she could surpass.
Her child's smile was her guiding light,
Each hurdle she faced was an opportunity to fight.

OVERCOMER

She dove into motherhood's deep, vast ocean,
Learning to swim with unyielding devotion.
In the depths of her heart, she found the strength,
To overcome stigma and society's relentless length.

COURAGE IN HER CHILD'S EYES

Her youth was a melody, disrupted but strong,
Her song, once off-key, now harmonious all along.
For she found courage in her child's eyes,
A love that would help her to rise.

TESTAMENT OF A WOMAN

With tender arms, she cradled her destiny,
A young mother torn, yet courageous, you see.
She nurtured a love so pure and true,
Her child's growth, a testament to the woman she grew.

JOURNEY OF UNKNOWN

Like an early bloom, she defied expectations,
A young lady who overcame limitations.
She persevered through a journey unknown,
For her child's future, a fierce love was sown.

THE POETESS STRENGHT

Her spirit soared high, overcoming doubts,
A young mother who embraced her unique route.
A soft touch, a guiding hand she did extend,
Her strength and resilience knew no end.

UNWAVERING DETERMINATION

From the depths of innocence, she rose,
A young woman whose strength only she knows.
With a child in tow, she faced each day,
Her unwavering determination leading the way.

OBSTACLES OF PAIN

She walked a path filled with obstacles and pain,
But from a young mother's heart, love did sustain.
Through days that felt heavy, nights long and weary,
She carried on, with unwavering bravery.

FIERCE FIRE

In her tender youth, the world misunderstood,
But within her, a fierce fire withstood.
She transformed her hardship into a powerful song,
A mother who proved society wrong.

A BEACON OF HOPE

Through teary nights and sleepless days,
Her love for her child never ceased to amaze.
From a young girl, she grew unapologetically strong,
A beacon of hope, a melody of overcoming wrong.

PATH UNKNOWN

She embraced motherhood, though young and afraid,
A brave soul who refused to let her dreams fade.
With each step, she forged a path unknown,
A young lady whose strength has since grown.

SOLACE AND PEACE

In her embrace, a child found solace and peace,
A young mother's love echoed and would never cease.
From the depths of despair, she emerged anew,
A lady who painted her own sky so blue.

STORM OF JUDGMENT

Amidst a storm of judgment and despair,
She stood proud, refusing to compare.
For she knew that her journey was her own,
A young mother whose love brightly shone.

STRENGHT

In her young eyes danced shades of experience,
A loving mother with wisdom immense.
Though she started her journey so young,
Her strength grew, with each song she sung.

A YOUNG MOTHER

Through trials and doubters that crowded her way,
She built a future brighter than they could portray.
A young mother who defied odds stacked high,
With her determination, she reached for the sky.

SEEDLING OF DOUBT

She danced to the rhythm of her own tune,
A young lady who weathered life's monsoon.
From a seedling of doubt, she grew tall and strong,
A mother who emerged triumphant, after so long.

VENTURED WITH GRACE

A story of resilience, a tale to be told,
Of a young lady who grew resilient and bold.
Through uncharted paths, she ventured with grace,
Transforming her pain into strength that embraced.

MICHELLE CITRON

STATE: NAVADA (LAS VEGAS)

COUNTRY: UNITED STATES/ PUERTO RICO

WHY DO YOU WRITE POETRY?

Poetry is an inherent part of my being, a calling from the depths of my soul to express through words. With poetry, I find myself immersed in the rhythm of syllables and the richness of symbolism, like dancing to a melody only I can hear.

In the vulnerability of poetry, I discover a profound sense of liberation. It becomes a canvas where I paint the messy yet beautiful tapestry of my life's experiences and perspectives. Life's juxtapositions of chaos and beauty are woven into every verse, forming a captivating dichotomy that I embrace wholeheartedly.

Growing up as a Puerto Rican in the Bronx exposed me to the harsh realities of poverty, violence, and despair. Yet, amidst the struggles, I found solace in the vibrant spirit of mi gente—the passion for art, music, dance, and storytelling. Poetry, for me, is the embodiment of this spirit—it is the song that resonates within my heart and the pathway to my soul's deepest expressions.

WHAT IS YOUR MESSAGE TO THE WORLD?

Life is a whirlwind of chaos and splendor, weaving together a magnificent tapestry of messy and breathtaking moments. In this intricate fabric of existence, let kindness illuminate your path because we all have a unique and compelling story deserving of empathy and understanding.

CHAPTER SEVEN
MICHELLE CITRON

ARE YOU THERE?"

Please don't leave my side
The plea of his inner child
"I won't," said I
I promised to be back in a while

I didn't want to go
Only needed a moment
To collect my broken heart
Watching him detox
The physical pain
Emotional torture
Loathing of himself
Too much to bear
I pleaded to God
Are you there?

"I'm back"
I announced with a smile
His tender eyes
The lost inner child
Arms extended out
"Mamma, please hold me
I'm afraid, I'm really scared
Not sure I have the fortitude
To see this thing through
Sorry if I disappointed you"
Thoughts in his child's mind

I took this child in my arms
Kissed his forehead
Held his convulsing body in my arms
Mamma is by your side
I have never stopped loving you
Perhaps you were lost for a while
Take my hand and let's be bold
This time you will kick the habit
I promise to never let you go

Sinking into theta state
He dreamed with angels
Who carried him through day by day
It's time to rest and forgive your past
Receive the blessings of the healing light
Rise dear son, stand on your feet
The time has come for you to defeat
Your demons and their limiting beliefs

Sleep my precious little one
Your transformation has begun
When you rise in the morning's dawn
A new beginning awaits
Untethered soul
Freedom is your place
Fly my lovely child
Allow your wings to spread
Life is at your fingertips
You only need believe
You are worthy of her grace

"Are You There?"
By Michelle Cintron

MOM, MAMÁ, MOTHER, MAMI

Being a Mom
The greatest love of all
We love with radical intensity

Being a Mom
The body's metamorphosis
I cocoon my beautiful butterfly

Being a Mom
Sleeplessness nights gazing at my baby's chest
Obsessively checking for their timely breath

Being a Mom
A strong desire to protect my children
As steps are designed for leaving the nest

Being a Mom
Carrying the weight of the world
As I smile through the challenges

Being a Mom
Takes outrageous courage and strength
As my heart sets off like fireworks

Being a Mom
My biggest legacy
The greatest love of all

"Being A Mom"
by Michelle Cintrón

"DEATH AT MY DOOR"

Death called upon me today
Gingerly knocking on my door
An invitation to come home
To cross the threshold
A field of source energy to explore
Me? Is it me you're calling for?
I am declining the generous offer
For the timeliness is an inconvenience
I have yet to fulfill all my life's promises
My family needs me
Clearly there must be room for negotiation
Isn't there someone else who could RSVP?
Please give me more time
I promise to be better, do more
Live my life's purpose as planned
My request is not about me you see
It's about all those dreams not realized
About all the people who need me
The lives of whom I still get to impact
I'm pleading, don't take me
I am regretfully declining your invitation
You can't possibly insist on taking me
How does this all work anyway?
Like a lottery, one in a million
And today is my lucky day

"Death At My Door"
By Michelle Cintron

"WOULD YOU LOVE ME?"

Would you love me if I shaved my hair?
Would you love me when I don't care?
Would you try to change my ways,
or leave me behind for better days?

Would you love me when I am scared?
Would you love me?
Do you dare?
Would you find the nearest escape?
Perhaps even turn love into hate.

Would you love me when I'm not my best?
Would you love me if I'm a hot mess?
Would you support me on a shitty day,
or walk away because it's easier that way?

Would you love me when my love is too much?
Would you love me and surrender to trust?
Would love be ludicrous based on your past?
Will you allow love in with hopes it will last?
Would you love me if I am far from perfect?
Would you love me or treat me like a reject?
Would you love me if they say I am a witch
or fear my intensity and leave without a hitch?

Would you love me? Could you love me?
Would you love me? Do you love me?
Would you allow me to teach you how?
Are you bolding enough to love me now?

"Would You Love Me?"
By Michelle Cintron

"I AM LIFE"

A flutter inside feels like a butterfly
Such begins this little and delicate life
Created from love, you come alive
Growing safely in my tummy
Nestled in this magical place called home
Feeding you from my heart and soul
I am the vessel for this perfect being
Waiting patiently for months to pass by
The time arrives to meet my precious one
It is the hardest journey I will take
From a small canal a wonder is born
Staring deeply into each other's eyes
I see your perfection and innocence
You are mesmerized by my divinity
Two souls United forever in time
Mother's Day poetry - In honor of all women

"I Am Life"
By Michelle Cintron

"A NOTE TO SUICIDE"

Dear Suicide,
You suck

Lost my loved one to your promise to end pain

Your allure to cure chronic grief and shame

You steal hope from the disheartened

Manipulation of the broken hearted

You suck

I hope you are happy with your army

of loved ones snatched too soon

Sucked into an abyss never again to be seen

Taken from families and friends

Fuck you suicide

You suck!

"A Note to Suicide"
by Michelle Cintrón

COVID-19

Anxiety in the present time
People trapped in scarcity
And feeling crazy
Has society lost its mind?

A tiny virus breeding fear
Incubating, terrorizing
Spreading like wildfire
Manipulating the human sphere
Bodies on fire
The infected gasp for air
Down to the wire
Does anyone care?

Isolation, quarantine
Secluded by hospital doors
No visitors allowed
Who will save me now?
Paralyzed by the loneliness
Human touch has dwindled
Poked and prodded by workers
Covered in gloves and PPE

On a mission to defeat Corona
It's invaded my body
Permeating, multiplying
Attacking my respiratory

Minuscule superpower triumphs
White robed professional
Seals my eyes shut
Declares my expiration

Lingering above the earthly vessel
The white light beckons from above
Illumination and ascension await
Time to return to thy natural state

COVID-19

By Michelle Cintron

"FEAR"

Fear has reared its ugly head
Dared me to fight, took me to bed
The allure so appealing to me
Gave a false sense of security

It hoisted me on its back
Cajoled me into a secret pact
Not aware of the path created
Self-sabotage was perpetrated

Trapped by this fury knowingly called fear
Masked by a cape I aimed to escape
Why a victim to this rape
Stripped and beaten to my demise
Loathing myself, I cannot rise

Stripped my power, down on my knees
Shame and guilt dangle like keys
Inserted in the ignition of my life
Driving force, bludgeoned by knife
Why do you mock my integrity
Relinquished power to sheer stupidity
Beaten, wounded, been knocked down

No redemption in sight, I lost my crown
Cracked knuckles, bruised face
How much longer on this race
Begging and pleading have mercy on me
Surrender to what is and set me free

"Fear"

By Michelle Cintron

CAITLIN WILCOX

COUNTRY: UNITED STATES

I am Caitlin. I'm in my mid-thirties.

WHY DO YOU WRITE POETRY?

I have traveled a path of pain and turmoil like so many. I have actively engaged in a healing process that has led to ascending into an enlightened state. It has been, and continues to be a difficult journey, but peace and love prevail.

WHAT IS YOUR MESSAGE TO THE WORLD?

It is my hope that this collection allows you to heal and connect to me and others who have traveled a difficult path. You are not alone and healing is within reach no matter how far down the trail of depravation you have gone, I am a being of light. But so are you. You are not alone.

CHAPTER EIGHT
CAITLIN WILCOX

LONE WOLF

All of the faces she sees every day
Smiling and waving them over her way
"How are you today, sir? It's so good to see you!"
And when she says this, her words- they are true
But somehow these moments with familiar faces
Don't quite add up to unclaimed embraces
For when she leaves there for her home destination
She's in for a long night of alienation
Although she is liked by many she knows
The lack of connection continues and grows
And though she has many people who call her their friend
The isolation feeling won't seem to end
She sits in her mind and imagines a place
Where she feels so connected and safe in her space
A world where the loneliness doesn't stack
Where she's part of the crew; not alone in the pack

By Caitlin Wilcox
@2021

BEEN THERE

I have been there.
In the depths of great despair
Running from myself, the truth,
Any inkling of such proof
That shows I'm not alone at all
Perhaps I'm wrong, I've just hit a wall
I have been there
In the depths of great despair
Feeling hopeless and afraid
Of what my life choices have made
Is there chance to rectify
I couldn't see it with my eye
I have been there
In the depths of great despair
Barely able to discern
The fact of temporary yearn
"This too shall pass" seemed quite untrue
I almost did what I couldn't undo
I have been there
In the depths of great despair
But now I'm not so I wanted to say
You too can hang on one more day
Life comes in cycles of good and bad
But I'll be here for you when you're depressed or sad.
Because I have been there.

By Caitlin Wilcox
@2021

TIME DIMMED LIGHT

The time; it is upon me
The whispers they do draw near
With words of evil folly
Singing self-hate in my ear
I long to comfort in the night
I long to feel the trace
Of luminescent, sure self
Love
And a god's forgiving grace
But as I sit within the hell
That I have self-created
I spin my saddest tale to you
Of why I feel devastated.
It all began so long ago
When I was but a child
Born to families on both sides
Their love was more than mild
But fate would have that my dear ma
Would pick the only one

Who harbors no love in his heart
His soul, devoid or numb.
So early in my childhood
I learned I'm not enough
No matter the love given by the rest
He hadn't time for us
So, when he finally, free from jail

Had option to engage
He chose to run and galivant
To a far away, southern state.
Now he's long gone and I am there
A teen with no self esteem
My depression hit the baseline
But my love and kindness gleamed.
I entered my religious era
Giving and taking in love

But no matter how much good I did
I never felt enough
Then I went to college
and I found some escape there.
No one faced emotions
Drugs and avoidance filled the air.
I met a guy who I thought loved me
Whose intellect was big as space
And I thought I was happy
Til he punched me in the face.
So, I fled from that chapter
Of my life and went back to start
My body young and pretty
Contrasting my broken heart
"It was then I met the man
Who would shape the next decade
Who left me in a puddle
With my heart in a barricade.
He showered me in ample love

Acceptance and in attention

He gave me all the things my heart
Had craved- my lifelong mission
Then I had my daughter
And things got kind of weird
His love and adoration
They quickly disappeared
He said to me, yes more than once
That he had felt unloved
So, in an effort to show him
I offered him my glove
He married me and then you'll see
A few years down the road
My belly swelled and time would tell
Our family had grown.
And by the time this perfect boy
Had come to join the scene
I was elated or so depressed

There was no in between.
The father of my children
And the husband I now had
His words would cut me like a knife
And leave me broken and sad
And by the time that boy was two
And our sweet girl was eight
My husband had the nerve to hit
More than a dinner plate.

And finally, I hit that point
Where I could take no more
I filed for protection
and I walk right out the door
I've since met up with oldest friend
and we became much more
Another bouncing baby boy
To add to my child score.
And this man, unlike the rest
His intentions are in grace
He tries to hold my heart
and bring a smile to my face.
But as I mentioned earlier
I'm not as I was before
I always end up shattered
Into pieces in the floor
And this dear friend and lover
He's left to hold the broom
He's doomed to sit and spend his life
In this shattered glass filled room
I'm triggered and I'm angry
And the place were light once sat
Is filled with hollow yearning
To simply have it back

By Caitlin Wilcox
@2023

SHE WAS SMILES

Silent wakeful darkest night
Bringing out my urge to fight
For when I sit alone with these
Intrusive thoughts and memories
Thinking of my many flaws
My huge mistakes and small faux pas.
Thinking of where I went so wrong
Within my life, though I thought I was strong
But in the ever-eternal night
I somehow fail to see my light
And all that I can do right then
Is let the demons' words pour in
Depression flows through every vein
And teardrops fall like heavy rain
Dwelling in my own despair
My past choices bring me there
So, when you see me in the light
Not shadowed by the evil night
Just know that I have been to hell
And that is why I treat you well.

By Caitlin Wilcox
@2023

DIVINE WISHES

In the air of the sanguine moonlight
I look upon my worries
And I gaze into the beauty
Of the fact that they are small
The reason for perception
Of minimizing consequence
Is the splendor of her glory
In this gorgeous breeze of fall
Worries, they consume us
Our spirits heavily hang

With bending nails in cracked up frames
Along our life path wall
And so, within the sacred night
With moon so full and ever bright
Shedding that which serves me not
That is my battle call
So, a blessing I send to you
Simply for having read my heart
That you may answer this summon
Into place May your life fall
Make way for all your blessing
By casting away the unwanted
May prosperity come to your home,
And your soul, again, hold all

By Caitlin Wilcox
@2023

IMAGINE

Imagine. A soul; ancient.
The construct of time has gifted the spirit
With rich experience- -
Abundant love-patience.
Imagine. This peaceful essence
Into the next cycle, then sent with a whirl
To experience life's full effervescence
the extremes to each end, 'round them whirl.
This light, now paired with an ego
And with it comes feelings, emotions so deep
That it's now hard to let go
And function without the impassioned steep.
All actions, now tainted.
By things perceived through a veil of sensation
Discord presented with full colors, painted
Creating deep rooted alienation
This being, once pure,
Emotion now pulling the strings of the show
As the luminosity dims ever more
And their energies gradually slow.
The light must cast aside its ego
I think that we all can agree
But the thing you probably don't know…
Is: the soul here- it's you, and it's me.

By Caitlin Wilcox
@2023

SHATTERED VASE

Negative feelings fill up my whole vessel.
With depressive thoughts I do once again wrestle.
Trauma, and hormones, and anxiety…
I am so overwhelmed; emotionally.
Surrounded by people and social inclusion
Yet all of that somehow feels
Like an illusion.
No one is here, for they can't understand.
I think my brains way is alone in this land….
Perhaps I've finally broken from my PTSD
Of abuses gone by… "ancient history"
Or so it would seem from outside looking in….
But if I close my eyes, it can all re-begin….
Did you ever think you're too broken to mend?
Like a vase made of crystal with platinum plated end?
It was priceless at one point; had so much to offer
But once it did shatter, it was worth not a dollar….

By Caitlin Wilcox
@2023

BROKEN

I'm Broken.
Angry words spoken.
Sanity taken.
Not strong; simply mistaken.
Brain damaged.
Triggers; unmanaged.
Unbalanced center.
No one should enter.
Another outburst.
These feelings; the worst.
Words spray outward.
But true feelings not heard.
Inner war zone.
I fight to reclaim home.
A place deep inside.
It continues to hide.
Time seems gone.
You, ready to move on.
But then I am left.
Just me in my mess.
My heart cries to you.
It says my love is true.
But no sadder words spoken.
Because, I am broken.

By Caitlin Wilcox
@2023

HEALING JOURNEY

I wish a wish with all my heart
For my whole world not to fall apart.
I suffer waves of pain and bliss
The bouts of yelling wouldn't be missed.
I cry and yell and then meditate
The centered moment, appreciate.
I feel the agony, the pain
The triggered reactions yield much shame
Medication, meditation
Feeling sad about my situation
Next thing you know, I'm up again
Trying hard, just know I can win
Then I'm down and so depressed
About myself, my life, this mess
I question all I am and then
I'm right back up, tip-top again
Is this the way the healing goes?
Or is it something no one knows?
Am I ok, or will I be?
Am I doomed to this atrocity?
I wish a wish to heal and grow
I wish it harder than you could know.
Perhaps one day I'll have my prize
And peace will settle deep inside.

By Caitlin Wilcox
@2023

FAR GONE

I'm making quite the mess
Out of my whole life
My "fight or flight" ain't right.
Someone pinches me, please.
Wake me from this sleep.
The nightmare can't go on.
I've lived it far too long.
Why do I react?
Instead of stepping back?
Anger grows so fast
From sadness and trauma past.
Here I go again.
Hating on my best friend.
He doesn't even see
How his actions hurt me.
Cause maybe I'm all wrong.
My hearts been hurt too long.
If he did the same to you…
You may not care, it's true.
But to me it's sharpened blade.
Cutting into my pain.
In an openly gushing fashion
Of my life before our passion.
How could he love me?
She of the misery…
My heart may be too smashed…
For inner peace to last.
Perhaps I've gone too far.
And there is no guiding star…
To lead me from this pain.
So I can be whole again.

By Caitlin Wilcox @2023

READY, SET... GROW!

Power shifting.
Vibrational lifting.
Source, Cosmos, God;
Whatever path you trod....
Ready to engage
Awaken loving age
Feel energy flow
Intuitions grow.
Fast upon me, came
This rising, heated flame
And it now accelerates
Ever closer to that place...
That place where I am me.
In pure divinity- and femininity
To cultivate my light
To sanctify the night...
To shed a glow now on

Things perceived- so wrong.
We must embrace our path.
For peace to one day last.
But many seek outside
What our inner selves confide
And conditioning takes grasp
And time moves far too fast.
So many haven't found
The amazing and beautiful sound

Of connecting to higher self
A world of spiritual wealth
But each blessing, I count
Gratitude is paramount.
And every day anew,
I'm thankful for the view....
So please come share in this
Exquisite contentedness
It's easier to grow
If you let your burdens go.

By Caitlin Wilcox
@2023

ONWARD

Growing ever weary
Of my inability
To see my future clearly
Infinite possibility.
I do very well one day
Then next day I do not.
I don't know what I can say
About those messy spots.
I guess, in part the problem
Is that I've been retrained.
It isn't conscious choice
But safety switch within my brain.
So how does one rewrite the code
Of virus, oh so vile?

Answer lies with ancient mode,
Meditative in its style.
I suppose I should remember
That it took time to unfold
So, I need time to encumber
This protective reflexive hold.
If I diligently practice
A meditative grace,
I will get the knack of
An enlightened, centered place.
So onward, upward I shall go,
and healing in times wake
A life of peace I'll have to show
For every effort I take.

By Caitlin Wilcox
@2023

HUNTER MOONS

The glow of the equinox;
Full circle illuminating the sky
She beckons hunters
To prepare for what lies ahead.
And they who wrap themselves up
In the veil between worlds through all seasons
Find themselves exposed
As garment becomes tenuous
And in the sacred moonlight
Bask in the council and wisdoms of those
With divine prudence

Rare as most precious astatine
"Hark!" The Hunter orb doth cry
"Prepare for respite; winter's inertia
Looming closer now. "
Speaking with absolution.
And with this command; promise
For, after the release of autumn kiss
Comes winters reprieve
Who gives to us time to reflect
When In the long winter months
We are granted the season to cast back
Things which do not serve
Preparing for spring renewal
So as autumn calls to shed
Our excess; take comfort in knowing that
It's sacred purpose
Is to cleanse our vessels for new.

By Caitlin Wilcox
@2023

DIVINE WISHES

In the air of the sanguine moonlight
I look upon my worries
And I gaze into the beauty
Of the fact that they are small
The reason for perception
Of minimizing consequence
Is the splendor of her glory
In this gorgeous breeze of fall
Worries, they consume us
Our spirits heavily hang
With bending nails in cracked up frames
Along our life path wall

And so, within the sacred night
With moon so full and ever bright
Shedding that which serves me not
That is my battle call
So, a blessing I send to you
Simply for having read my heart
That you may answer this summon
Into place May your life fall
Make way for all your blessing
By casting away the unwanted
May prosperity come to your home,
And your soul, again, hold all

By Caitlin Wilcox
@2023

THE HURDLE

The line sits empty.
The leaves said goodbye
It is too cold outside
To hang clothes out to dry.
I've shed all the things
That I no longer need
And now I feel empty
I'm a whole different breed
Now it would seem
My heart lives by the time
Of mother earths aging
Her ever-perfect design…
But I haven't quite mastered
The Art of self-love
So, emptiness doesn't
Sit snug like a glove.

Instead, I can feel
Every empty, cold space.
And I yearn to put
Loving vibes in that place.
It is hard to accept
My next path to trod
For without revelation
I already was odd
So, I have this deep fear
Of alienation

As I step ever closer
To soul destination
I know there's a point
when the masses won't relate
To my thoughts, to my mind
And they won't appreciate

Who I am, why I love
And I won't feel the pull
Of deepest connection
With another Earthen soul
And in theory they say
That I won't miss it then
Being on like page
Of women and men.
But at present I'm scared
And I know I must go
To the places above
To the places below.
So, I rest for a moment
and prepare for a shift
As I move one step closer
To enlightenments lift.

By Caitlin Wilcox
@2023

GOOD MORNING

Awake. Finally awake.
From this life I now will take
All the wealth I'm offered out
But, see I'm not talking about…
Money, gems, gold or gifts
In the physical sense of this…
But in a much more radiant tone
The gift of joy, of love, of home.
And of the new ability
To see my world with clarity.
And though our viewpoints mightn't align

I know that will change with some span of time.
And maybe it won't be in this place or life
But our journey expands on both ends of this strife.
I see bigger picture, as always, I have
But now it is broader and I'm really quite glad.
I live in a place between what you may know
And the garden from whence our whole universe grows
It isn't surprising you think me quite odd
You can't see the whole of me from the path you now trod.
But I do assure you you're rather strange too
If you could see the whole being of you.
But that my dear friend may be for later date
So, until then, my loves, your blessings-appreciate.

By Caitlin Wilcox
@2023

I'VE MISSED YOU

My soul calls out to yours.
Like a mother calling home her child.
It relentlessly implores
With its soft, commanding style.
"Please connect to me"
It cries out to each small piece.
"Without you, I'm incomplete
And this longing shall not cease"
I work with diligence
To ready my spirit for a time
To experience emergence
All soul shards collected, the feeling sublime.
Across the planes
Of galactic proportion I fly
But I still feel the strains
Of everyday problems and earthy life
But as forward I delve
The winds of the universe clear the debris
My emotional well
I find always full; no longer empty.

By Caitlin Wilcox
@2023

SUPERPOWER

Love is my super power
Dormant it lay for decades
Until the perfect hour
To let it be displayed.
Before I was yet able
To yield unending light
I had many battles
I fought many a fight.
But now all of those struggles
Are vanishing at last
I no longer am tethered
To my painful past.
Inward I was forced to go
And inward, then I went.
And now all of my love does flow
.
My true enlightenment.
The path to self is scary.
The path to self is painful.
But it is worth most every step
To sing amongst the angels.
So, I send this blessing out,
That you may also know.
The true abundance in self-love
That enlightened, eternal flow.
I wish for you internal peace
And connection with higher you.
I pray for your acceptance
To let your heart stay true.
For if you let your love flow in,
It will then flow back around.
And you can have super powers too.
And inner peace abounds.

MOTHER MOON

On the last full moon of twenty23
In Cancer she sat and beamed down.
I was given some blessings I hadn't foreseen
As clouds covered and rain drizzled down.
I woke from a slumber, a deep short sleep
I felt emotional swell in my soul
I was greeted with calm to my rage-Ish peak
And I felt ever out of control.
My moon water out, though I'd not touched it yet.
The kitchen sits clean from a meal I didn't cook.
So, in effort to calm, I went out in the wet
Knowing clouds would make it hard to have a look.
I set my conscious on my own mind
And located the bright patch of cloud
And as I began to meditate, I did find

That the wisps were all moving around.
As I said my first "ohm" and I grounded my vessel
I set my gaze up to the skies.
And with second breath in, I could see the veil rustle.
And it parted as though for my eyes.
The orb of December shown down on my soul
And she spoke to me loud and quite clear
I gazed on her beauty, in love shining-full
As she said what I needed to hear.
She told me be grateful for all that I have.
She said that more blessings will flow
She told me that I must continue my path
And remember always for love's light to show.
I listen with gratitude, humble and true
Laid bare to her wisdom of old.
I prepare for my life to start fresh and start new
And she knows that I'll do what I'm told.

WARRIOR OF LIGHT

To give yourself to someone else
It leaves you vulnerable.
To have your heart then places on a shelf….
The feeling is intolerable.
But then you add the hateful words
You add the rage and screams
And in the eyes where love once sat
An evil demon gleams.
Then some time on down the road
You deal the strain of hate
And then the physical side takes hold
Leaves you in bruised up state.
So finally, you break the chains
Of toxic trauma bond
And you then think you're fine to start
To retry loves coat on

It all starts great but sooner than not
A bouncing baby boy
Joined my lovely children
Bringing smiles love and joy.
Unfortunately, for me you see…
His father didn't align.
He was stuck within the path
Of cyclic addictive crime
So, then I now have opened up
My heart to two, not one

And having it repeatedly smashed
Is quite some less than fun.
The week then came for me to find
Three huge revelations.
It was the type of thing that shakes

The hearts of every nation
One was secret text messages
To someone who did me way wrong
Then there was the drinking
And a call that sang betrayals song.
And then the last and final straw,
if this was not enough,
Then I "accidentally"
Got picture messages and stuff.
The image showed that I had never
Mattered to him at all
The third and final strike -
Invoked my battle call.
So now I will stand victorious
Atop a battleground
When all I ever wanted
Was to give my love in bounds….

By Caitlin Wilcox
@2023

YOU HAVE ONE UNREAD MESSAGE.

"Hark!" I hear my soul cry out.
"Inner changes must come about.
Effervescent, radiant light
Must shine within on darkest night"
And so, I inward delve, and now
I resurface and take a bow.
I found forgiveness and self-love,
My spirit soars in the skies above....
It was a path with many trials
Wading rushing water for miles
But every step my heart did take
Brought me closer to meditative state
And once I reach my darkest depths,
My heart bled out,
My eyes, they wept.
But once the pain was ushered out
Change began to come about.
And now my traumas are all but gone
My heart sings self-love in her song
And as I gaze on Earth, anew,
My higher self now beckons you
Join the fight and reply to the call
Enlightenment is for us all.
If you wish for peace and bliss
Internal peace is the answer to this.
I know that many have far to trod
And the journey to self is rattled with "odd"
But I can assure you it's worth the trip
To join me in Enlightenment's grip.

By Caitlin Wilcox
@2023

PRAYER OF MANIFESTATION

I call upon the universe
With all my heart and soul
To usher in my highest path
To heal and make me whole.
I ask for blessings of many type
Health, love, money and peace
I pray all inner turmoil
Suddenly does cease.
I ask for clearest guidance
From that higher intellect
I pray I have the faith to go
And not to sit and dissect.
I call all of my sacred
DNA right back to me
I ask that it infuse me

With pure divinity
I call upon the feminine
And masculine Divine
To finish up the healing
Of my heart and of my mind.
For I have come so far so fast
And self-love I have found
But I've a few more waves to treed
Before I find dry ground.
So dearest parent universe
And to highest self, I call
Bring all of my blessings round.
I'm ready for them all.
I thank you in advance
Because I know that it is done
Because you are a part of me
And in you, we all are one.

RUTH NAMATOVU

COUNTRY: UGANDA

WHY DO YOU WRITE POEMS?

I write poems because it allows me to express ideas and emotions in a creative and artistic way, showcasing the versality of language and engaging with users on a more imaginative level.

WHAT IS YOUR MESSAGE TO THE WORLD?

My message to the world is one of understanding, empathy, and collaboration, through open communication and shared knowledge, we can work together to build a better future for everyone. Just be who you are. There is no one better than you.

CHAPTER NINE
RUTH NAMATOVU

I AM A SINNER

I fell in love with a king
Whose love would never sting
Whose finger wore my ring
Whose lips "forever my love" would sing
Whose heart my love would bring
But I, a commoner sinned
I sinned against his love indeed.
His love was all I needed I won't deny
Too perfect to dry
Yet so sad his intentions were not love
And me a sinner felt I was flying like a dove
So, I, a commoner sinned.
But what did I get in the end?
What did I get u say indeed.
I got peace when I left his heart
And so much to testify that I can sleep at night

WHERE ARE THEY?

Those that promised good without hesitation
And greed was never their intention.
Where are they?
Those that fought for justice
And in their protests, we said our trust is.
Where are they?
Those that put their countrymen first
And never would they on the list be last.
Where are they son?
Are they hiding in holes of deep truth
Or watching us in through their curtains so smooth?
Should we cry out for their help
Or stay silent watching them take another step?
To our everlasting suffering we stand
Cheers to us for lifting disaster for our land!

©®RUTH

HEAR ME OUT MY LOVE

I'm the moonlit dance, two hearts entwine,
A timeless love, a tale divine.
Whispers soft, like a gentle breeze,
Eternal vows made under starry seas.

Through seasons changing, love remains,
A melody sweet, no hint of strains.
Hand in hand, through joy and sorrow,
Their love, a promise for tomorrow.

In twilight's glow and morning light,
They paint a canvas, pure and bright.
A symphony of love, a timeless song,
Forever bound, where they belong.

Through every trial, they find their way,
Love's compass guiding, night and day.
With each heartbeat, a love reborn,
In this timeless tale, forever sworn.

©®RUTH

ETERNAL MEMORY OF US

Beneath the silvered sky, our love unfolds,
A dance of souls, where passion molds.
Your laughter, a melody in the air,
In this sweet embrace, we have our share.

Through valleys deep and mountains high,
Together we soar, our spirits nigh.
In every beat, our hearts entwine,
A love so rare, forever thine.

As time unfolds its endless art,
You're the lyrics to my beating heart.
In this symphony of love, we'll play,
Eternally bound, come what may.

©®RUTH

WHERE IS THE LAUGHTER?

In a home where laughter once held sway,
Families shared joy in the light of day.
Around the table, they used to dine,
Smiles and laughter, a cherished sign.

But shadows crept in, and joy took flight,
The warmth of laughter turned to night.
Echoes lingered, faint and worn,
In the silence, a family mourned.

They searched for laughter, lost, unseen,
Wondering where joy had ever been.
In the fragments of a broken bond,
They sought the laughter that had abscond.

©®RUTH

IS THIS THE REAL ME?

In a world of whispers and expectations,
A girl sought answers, faced tribulations.
Choices lingered, a crossroads displayed,
Between conformity and her own way.

Society's canvas painted with hues,
She wrestled with paths she didn't choose.
Crafted by voices, molding her form,
Yet inside, a rebellion, a quiet storm.

Fingers pointed, words etched in air,
Yet within her, a spirit rare.
To conform or rebel, the struggle within,
A quest for self in a world so thin.

In the dance of shadows and societal plea,
She pondered, "Is this the real me?"
For in her heart, a desire stood,
To embrace her truth, to be understood.

©®RUTH

WHERE ARE THEY?

In lands of the old, where heroes tread,
Fought valiantly for our land, it is said.
In love, they embraced the soil so dear,
Awake they slept, guarding without fear.
East and west, they roamed with pride,
Home, the anchor, where hearts reside.
In sacrifice, they chose to make a stand,
For the future of their grandchild's land.
Yet, today, where do they hide?
Amidst the changes, where do they bide?
Our land trembles, cries for a guiding hand,
A savior to rise, to protect and withstand.
Let their spirits awaken once more,
To restore what's lost, to mend the core.
For our land, now in distress,
Needs heroes again, to redress.

©®Ruth

THAT IS WHO I AM

Under Uganda's skies, where the equator divides,
I am the rhythm in the valleys, where the spirit resides.
In the pearl of Africa's embrace, where Victoria roars,
I am the essence of a nation, united by ancient shores.

From Rwenzori's heights to the Sipi Falls cascade,
I am the heartbeat of Uganda, in every serenade.
In the warmth of smiles, beneath banana leaves' shade,
I am "That is who I am," in the stories portrayed.

On the shores of Lake Bunyonyi, where whispers linger,
I am the echo of gorillas and the song of the river.
In the tapestry of cultures, diverse and grand,
I am the soul of Uganda, in the heart of the land.

©®Ruth

UNBROKEN ECHOES

In a home where love once brightly gleamed,
A silent fracture, dreams once deemed.
Mother and father, now worlds apart,
Aching echoes, a shattered heart.

Yet in the midst of this quiet storm,
A girl, in innocence, takes on the norm.
Her prayers like whispers, soft and sincere,
Yearning for unity, wiping each tear.

Every night, under the moonlit dome,
She prays for a place she can call home.
In her heart, a plea, steadfast and true,
For her family's reunion, old bonds renew.

For she knows a journey lies ahead,
A path where her footsteps may be led.
Tradition's call, a daughter's fate,
Yet she dreams of a united, undivided state.

In the echo of prayers, a hope so grand,
That love might triumph, hand in hand.
Though her own path may soon unfold,
She dreams of a home that won't grow old.

A TALE OF HOPE

In a quiet place where kids say mean things,
there's a girl feeling really alone.
Her mom and dad aren't together now,
and school is tough, with a hurtful tone.

But in her heart, a little light stay, a hope that things might change,
She dreams of happy days,
where her family's love won't rearrange.

Sometimes, she cries when no one's near,
but she won't give in to sorrow,
In her heart, she believes in tomorrow,
dreaming of a better tomorrow.

Through the tough times, she stays strong, like a tiny, bright star,
Hoping that her mom and dad might find a way back,
no matter how far.

©®RUTH

TEARS ECHOING THROUGH THE NIGHT

In the quiet of the night, her cries pierce through the air,
A girl, tears streaming, burdened by a weight she cannot bear.
Her heart aches, echoes of a love lost in the shadows,
Whispers to the heavens, where her pain sadly grows.

"I miss you," she sobs, her voice a desperate plea,
Invisible chains tethering her to a love she can't set free.
Alive, yet distant, he dwells in the realm of the unknown
She yearns for his presence, in the emptiness of space.

Every tear, a testament to the void deep inside,
Aching for the one she loves, with nowhere to hide.
Daily, she cries to God, a prayer etched in despair,
Begging for the return of the one whose absence she can't bear.

Alive, but not beside her, his absence feels so real,
She longs for his laughter, the warmth only he could instill.
In the solitude of her tears, she reaches for the divine,
Hoping against hope that the missing piece will soon align.

MY LETTER TO YOU

In dreams, our love shines bright,
Like stars dancing in the night.
Your eyes, like the endless sky,
Hold my heart, never say goodbye.

Your words are like a sweet song,
Promising love that's forever strong.
Through all seasons, we'll be fine,
Our love's like a blooming vine.

Beneath the moon, our love story goes on,
Like a precious treasure, never gone.
Your laughter is like a happy song,
When I'm with you, nothing feels wrong.

As the sun sets, our love takes flight,
Growing stronger, reaching new height.
Sweet words between us, soft and neat,
With you, each moment is a sweet treat.

In the calm night, when shadows appear,
Our love stays strong, conquering fear.
So, here's my letter, honest and true,
Forever and always, I'm yours, it's true.

MAMA'S ENDLESS LOVE

When you talk about love, my mom's the key,
Warm and caring, like a lullaby for me.
Our bond is special, beyond compare,
Through bright days and nights so rare.

Love's a light that guides our way,
Sweet memories make our moments stay.
Quiet tunes play, like a steady beat,
Her love, a mystery that's truly sweet.

Her heart's like gold, a hidden find,
A love that's boundless, one of a kind.
Together through joy and wiping tears away,
Her love's a mystery, but here to stay.

©®RUTH

"HARMONY OF HERITAGE"

Beneath the acacia's shade, whispers unfold,
Histories untold in the warmth they hold.
Sweeping savannahs, where spirits reside,
Footprints linger, a journey to confide.

In ancestral rhythms, resilience beats,
Harmony forged, where destiny meets.
Rivers narrate tales of struggles faced,
Yet hope springs eternal, never erased.

Sunset hues paint a canvas of pride,
Unity blossoms, like the Baobab's wide.
Cultures entwined in a vibrant embrace,
African essence, a timeless grace.

©®RUTH

ULA DOUGLASS

COUNTRY: SPAIN

CHAPTER TEN
ULA DOUGLASS

"A BIT OF ME"

'The heart of alpujarra - Albondón' collection'

Poetry and mountains
Are so closely interwoven
Because the big things
The things that make us happy
Are as deeply etched in our souls
As mountains are fused in the land

The daily beauty of the landscape
Imprinted in my vision
One I see even when I close my eyes
Nothing can erase you
And that makes a bit of me
immortal
Immortal
in your endless beauty

"THE BEST OF US IS OUR SUM"

'The heart of alpujarra - Albondón' collection'

Together we can be

The strength of the nature

The soul of the land

Of this little earthly paradise

Here, in the soil below our feet,
the one that gives fruit despite the draught

Our LOVE is its beauty

And only by our goodness

Of joint forces and best intentions

Little amazing things do happen

And when we will be gone,

Buried,

In our big, small hopes

In our tiny braveries

Something good will be left behind

And that is

all that matters

"THE HEART OF ALPUJARRA"

Albondón' collection'

Being woken up by sorrowful howls of dogs, in complete darkness
way before the sunrise
Remembering that when I open my door
I'm in the middle of mountains & fields
Uninhibited nooks & crannies of the lands
Wildly populated with jewels of nature
Feels me with so much joy
That not much else matters anymore

THE NIGHTFALL

"The heart of alpujarra - Albondón' collection"

Here, on top of my little
Mountain
Where I dug the soil
To a make a little patio
Here is buried my soul
Full of the deepest
Emotions, surfaced by
The beauty of the view
The beauty of the land
Let me lie here in peace
When my time comes
Lord of
Infinite spaces
Let them burry
My strength of feelings
Here,
Where they belong.

BLESSING ADEBOLA

COUNTRY: NIGERIA

WHY DO YOU WRITE POETRY:

To bring smiles to the faces of the masses that there is still hope for the upcoming generation and using poetry to advocate tolerance.

CHAPTER ELEVEN
BLESSING ADEBOLA

SNOW WHITE

Have traveled far and wide
Across the Globe, Across the bridges
Fasten my eyes across the sea
Closer! Nearer! Afar
How soon will it be till I see the downpour of it
Not a glimpse
Not a shadow
Still waiting for a downpour
Various Festive were destroy but non like the Snow White.

The lines and space make me linger for more, that I have to still hold on to my pen but nothing coming to the box just have to drop the pen and jump in bed.

Excitement filled my heart when I saw the heavy downpour through the window, could this be a snow white I said to myself

I jump up from bed wipe my face thrice short the door behind, saw the children from the next door with the Snow White wishing themselves Merry Christmas as well exchanging cards with themselves, so it's Christmas! WOW! can't keep it to myself all I could do was dancing any beat without Santa singing.

I brought out my phone to message my friends and family telling them merry Christmas; First person to wish Merry C

"DANCING BEE"

Hop! Hop! Hop! Hop
Dancing Bee
Dancing Bee
Flying all around.
Singing a song of melody
How it hunts and bites,
with a honey in it tail.

"LITTLE FINE FOWL"

Little fine fowl
White little fine fowl
Sitting on a fence
Shaking it tail
Spreading it wings
White little fine fowl.

"DRUM STICK"

The Drum Stick
One bell gives a sound,
Two bells give another sound.
Is the beat coming from me
It gets to my heart.
What a flexible heart it is
That pump so high of it
No wonder the heartbeat keeps ticking
If I did know the drum stick
Could have been broken and shattered one
I wouldn't go for it.
What a pretty and golden sticks you her
But I wouldn't go for you.

"VISIBILITY"

A little lady!
All alone with his imagination of thought,
Starring close to the universe
All alone with different picture.
Flipping through his cumbersome heart of love.

Will my eyes be open to see myself on the platform?
He said to himself.
How can I come out of this hut of thought
My heartbeat of what awaits me.

Starring close to the universe
Different colors, large and small
Will I be seen;

echoes! echoes! echoes!
You can't be visible
You are just a little lad
Who still needs to be tutored.

I dream in colors.
When time calls for me
Dropping the voices of different shapes and cultures,
Standing firm on the platform of courage,
Speaking to numerical and alphabetical lines of space.

Not a mirror,
Not an imagination,
All in one-fold of visibility got me known.

"One day I will leave this world"

One day I will leave this world
With my deep wounds
And it will be a matter of a second

One day I'll make my own way
Then the memories will stay with me forever
They will substitute and even after tomorrow
May the world welcome me with both hands
I like this world full of humans

When I will leave…
I would like everything to go well
I would like to see the world differently

Knowing that all my wishes have a tomorrow

When I leave, I would like:
Let there be no more wars or pain
May my departure not bring misfortune

That I don't regret anything and I'm already getting over it

I will leave far from you and everyone
I will leave myself to shopping time

I will leave one day with my wounds
I will protect from cracks without breaks

I will do without a thousand regrets so
as not to leave room for a single secret

I will cover myself with infinite and eternal love

When I leave, I will remember all these

moments as if they were yesterday

I will fight to show you how proud I was of it too

When I leave this world,

I will live in the depths of your thoughts
I will transfer your reactions
The positive payment of your shares
I will be at the center of your decisions

You will feel me close but from afar
You will protect my images with care
Sometimes you will miss me more and less
One day my breath will mark its point

From there I will only exist in your hearts
I'll leave here with every one of my gray fears
When I leave, I will be judged less and taken badly.
I will just be in the angel, far from the events of the crisis

There's nothing sublime about a departure, it's just a surprise.

When I leave, ... I will leave!

OCEANIA LUSHAY SMITH

19yrs old

LITTLE ROCK ARKANSAS

COUNTRY: UNITED STATES

WHY DO YOU WRITE POETRY:

Poetry has a unique ability to encapsulate our feelings and experiences, conveying them in ways that ordinary language cannot. It reaches deep within our souls, touching upon the very essence of our being. It is through poetry that we find solace, understanding, and an unwavering sense of connection with others who have gone through similar struggles. One of the reasons poetries resonates with me so deeply is its ability to transcend barriers. It speaks to the hearts of individuals from all walks of life, regardless of their race or past experiences. It reminds us that no matter what challenges we have faced, we are capable of overcoming them and achieving greatness. Poetry empowers us to believe in ourselves and strive for a better future.

In my own journey, poetry has been a constant companion. It has provided me with a unique outlet to express my emotions and reflect on my past experiences. From the depths of love to the darkness of drugs and gang violence, poetry has allowed me to channel my pain and transform it into something beautiful. It serves as a reminder that I am not defined by my past, but rather by my ability to rise above it.

Moreover, poetry has given me the opportunity to connect with others who have walked a similar path. It has allowed me to create empathy and understanding, fostering a sense of community and kinship. Through my words, I aim to inspire and be an example to others, especially children, who may be going through their own struggles. By sharing my story, I hope to show them that they too can overcome obstacles and emerge stronger than ever. Poetry has become a mirror of my own journey, reflecting the highs and lows, the triumphs and tribulations. It has given me a voice when I felt unheard, and it continues to be a source of healing and growth. Through poetry, I have discovered the power of resilience, hope, and the endless possibilities that lie within each and every one of us.

So, dear friend, this is why I love poetry. It is a beacon of light in the darkness, a testament to the strength of the human spirit. It speaks to our shared humanity and offers a roadmap for those who may need guidance. May we continue to find solace and inspiration in the beauty of poetry, and may it always remind us that we are capable of accomplishing anything we set our minds to.

CHAPTER TWELVE
OCEANIA LUSHAY SMITH

GLORY

In this cold world we call our own we want
peace and a change to come on how we seek
for help and want to know will pain and darkness
reside how can we cope if we can't get along shake
each other hand and heal others broken souls

A call for glory, so desperate, so wide,
Children dying, tears falling like rain,
Police brutality causing endless pain.
Poverty and violence, a bleak reality,
Young ones filled with anger and hostility,
Wars and shit we don't know what's going
on hearing it's ok just move on

Bloods and crips, vice lords and other gangs,
A divided society where hope barely hangs.
killing our own kind that's very insane we
supposed to get along laughing and hanging
but we can't because we out here hating teaching
the young kids it's ok to be slanging

Men, lead the way, guide with compassion
teach our children violence is not the answer
hold their hand kiss them goodnight love and
cherish and show them real life teach the women
it's ok to cry hold them tight show them they
matter show them life and let their wisdom guide you right

And women, teach the world a different kind of
fashion open up and learn how to stop being so
sassy hold your head up lead the way teach
our kids' drugs are not ok teaching and help the men
knowledge and wisdom that we have and buried
inside love one other and show pure sight

Let's gather the broken, heal their wounds,
Listen to their voices, their thoughts in monsoons,
For we never truly know, the battles they fight,
The darkness they face, hidden out of sight.
Let parents sit down, talk to their young,
Show them the path where violence is shunned,
Teach them to lead, inspire and dream,
To rise above hatred, to let love redeem
No need we hurting and pleading for a change to
come hold a hand and lead the way help the
poor to see a brighter day as we lay and hurt
in sorrow forgive others for the hope of
tomorrow show one another that it's ok to take
a hand and lead each other every way and everyday

Oh, how we cry glory for someone to hear us
whole story as we come in peace and harmony,
we must believe we will achieve and be freed

BRIGHTER DAY

In a world where young lives are lost,
Where violence takes its dreadful cost,
Families and friends torn apart,
We must unite, let love restart.

Parents, sit down, converse with care,
Engage your children, be aware,
Teach them violence has no place,
In a world where empathy should embrace.

Let's come together, as one we stand,
To break the cycle, hand in hand,
It's not okay to follow that way,
Teach our children to lead and convey.

Listen, children, speak your truth,
Express your feelings, break the booth,
For in their minds, we may not see,
The pain they bear, the agony.

Poverty and gang violence prevail,
But gangs were meant to uplift, not assail,
To build, to lead, to guide the way,
Not spread destruction, but hope's array.
Don't blindly follow, don't sag your pride,
Lead with compassion, let love reside,
Show our youth that unity transcends,
The choices we make, the paths we blend.
Rape and bullying should never be,
Let's protect our children, set them free,
Encourage them to stand up and fight,
For justice and equality's light.

Running away, dropping out of school,
Are cries for help, a desperate duel,

Let's guide them back, provide support,
To empower their dreams, a life to court.

Burying our children, a pain so deep,
Let's hold them close, their memories we keep,
We need to come together, as people, as kin,
To heal the wounds that lie within.

Gangs weren't meant for war, but to restore,
To build, to lead, to guide and explore,
It's okay to have adversaries, it's true,
But let's find common ground, a different view.

We need God's grace, to quell the strife,
To overcome darkness, embrace a new life,
Put the guns down, let peace be found,
For we bleed the same, on common ground.

No such thing as black or white,
We're all human, let's end the fight,
Racism must wither, let equality bloom,
Let queens wear their crowns, dispel the gloom.
Let kings hold the torch, strong and bright,
Unite as one, ignite the light,
Bloods, Crips, Vice Lords, Gods and other gangs let's cease,
The violence, find harmony and peace.

In the end, it's love we need,
To heal the wounds, to truly succeed,
Together, we can overcome the strife,
And let goodness prevail, enriching life now I say it's going to be brighter day.

A POETESS DREAM

In a world where doubts may arise,
I told myself to reach for skies.
With pen in hand, my words would flow,
A poet's soul, In the depths of your soul, a fire ignites,
A poet's heart, shining through the night.
With words that flow like a gentle stream,
You paint a picture, ready to show.

People say they can't look away,
As they gaze into my eyes, they say.
For deep within, my soul a poet's dream.
I told myself, "I'll be the next Mya",
With verses that touch hearts, like a sweet aria.
In the eyes of all who see does reside,
An old soul, with wisdom and pride.

Embracing all that life may bring,
I bring forth positive energy, I sing.
Through storms and trials, I stand tall,
A 19-year-old, enduring it all.

Strength courses through my veins,
Resilience fuels my fiery flames.
Though challenges may try to test,
your grace,
They can't help but stare, in awe of your embrace.
For you possess an old soul, wise and true,

A depth of understanding, beyond just a few.
Your journey may be tough, filled with strife,
But your strength shines bright, through every life.

At only nineteen, you face each storm with might,
An inspiration, a beacon in the darkest night.
Your positive energy, a wellspring I rise above, surpassing the rest.

So let my poems be a testament,
To the power within, the light I've sent.
For age is just a number, they say,
And I am proof that strength finds its way.

No matter what obstacles I face,
I'll continue to embrace my grace.
For I am strong, beyond my years,
And through it all, I'll conquer my fears. of light,
Radiates warmth, and makes everything right.
So, hold your head high, dear friend so bold,
Embrace every challenge, as stories unfold.
For you are strong, resilient, and brave,
A warrior poet, to conquer and save.
OH, how this is a poetess dream

PUT THE GUNS DOWN

In a world where young ones fall, their lives taken away,
We mourn the loss, as darkness holds sway,
Families and friends, ripped apart by pain,
Parents must sit down, their children's hearts to gain.

Coming together as one, learning it's not okay,
To choose violence, to let innocence stray,
Children must listen, and speak their truth,
For in their minds, battles waged in their youth.

Poverty and gang violence, a vicious cycle to break,
Parents must stay close, their children's footsteps to take,
Teach them to lead, to rise above the fray,
To build, to guide, to find a better way.

No more sagging, no more superficial divide,
Love must unite, no matter what's inside,
Just because parents may choose a certain path,
Doesn't mean their children must follow in wrath.

Show them it's okay to hurt, and to heal,
To find strength within, to rediscover zeal,
Rape and bullying, tragedies we must address,
Protect the young, let their lives be blessed.
Running away, dropping out of school's embrace,
We must guide them back, their potential we won't erase,
No more burying our kids, the pain so deep,

Let's come together, in our hearts, let's keep.

As people, as one, we must unite,
In the face of adversity, we'll find the light,
Gangs weren't meant for war, but to build and guide,
To uplift, to inspire, to walk side by side.

It's okay to have foes, but let hatred subside,
Embrace forgiveness, let love be our guide,
God's presence we need, to conquer the devil's sin,
Lay down the guns, let peace and harmony begin.

Black or white, we're all made of the same,
Bleeding the same color, no need for blame,
Racism must cease, let equality reign,
Queens wear their crowns, kings hold the torch, unchain.

Bloods, crips, vice lords, and other gangs,
Let's find common ground, where harmony hangs,
For we are all God's children, made whole,
Lead with courage, never falter, never fold.

Show one another, it's okay to feel,
To pray as a family, love as our shield,
Stand up, stop fighting, let go of grudges tight,
Steal not from each other, love's flame ignites.

Let's not let one another down, in moments of need,
Extend a helping hand, teach, guide, and lead,

Respect and cherish women, let their worth shine,
Heal their wounds, let love intertwine.

Women, rise as leaders, raise the next generation,
Stop the gossip, the fights, the painful frustration,
Speak, communicate, let unity prevail,
Lead with strength, let wisdom set sail.

Open your third eye, let your vision expand,
Plant seeds of hope, in this tumultuous land,
Have faith, have wisdom, as Tupac once said,
Keep your head up, better days lie ahead.

Teach them well, let them lead the way,
In the footsteps of Martin Luther King, we'll stay,
Come together as one, like Michael Jackson's plea,
For change starts with us, let love set us free.
PUT THE GUNS DOWN

VOICE OF INNOCENT

In a world so cruel, where innocence is lost,
A tragedy unfolds, a heartbroken cost.
A mother's love shattered, her child taken away,
By an unknown killer, their life cut astray.

In the depths of her sorrow, she finds no reprieve,
As questions plague her mind, too many to conceive.
No answers to be found, only confessions of despair,
The pain and fear consume her, it's more than she can bear.

Waking up the next morning finding her child no
longer the clothes the shoes will always remain in
pairs leaving the memoirs of him or her it still remains

Tears stream down her face, a never-ending tide,
Forced to witness her beloved child's tragic demise.
Oh, how we must stop this senseless killing spree,
No more waking up to find our little ones lying dead, you see.

Let us unite against this unhappiness and strife,
Protecting the innocent, giving them a chance at life.
For every baby, precious and small,
Deserves love and safety, one and all.

WARRIORS OF LIFE

Envious souls, they draw near,
Believing riches bring no fear,
But when the storm of life descends,
Their toughness fades and pretense bends.
If my bag they wish to claim,
I'll wish them luck their own game,
Ungrateful beings, blind and cold,
Devoid of gratitude, so bold.

My friend, how could I let them slither,
Like snakes, they tried to make me wither,
But true strength lies within my soul,
And vengeance, now, shall take its toll.

You're a coward, weak and small,
Black folks rise above them all,
Together, united, our spirits high,
We'll show the world, we won't comply."

With each word, the human finds release,
Embracing power, declaring peace,
I listen to, understand the true,
Offering guidance, always there to.

In this moment, young pregnant teens I connect,
Creating art, in words select,
For through poetry, emotions flow,
And together they embrace, as time does go.

A LOVE'S RESURGENCE

Controlled by my thoughts, my mind deceived,
Wishing for an end, to no longer believe.
Yet, in this darkness, there lies a hope,
For within my soul, strength will elope.

Love was given, genuine and real,
But reciprocation, alas, failed to unveil.
You thought you knew how it would unfold,
Yet, their love for me remained untold.

A one-sided affection, a sour taste,
Promises broken, emotions misplaced.
Playing with my heart turned to a dangerous game,
Leaving scars and memories to blame.

But fear not, my dear soul, for time will mend,
For the heartache, it too shall transcend.
In future days, love will find its way,
And happiness will dawn, a brighter day.

So, hold on tight and keep faith alive,
For our love's journey, it will revive.
Though paths may change and feelings sway,
Hope remains, guiding my pure soul each day.

©Oceania Smith

"JOURNEY BACK TO LOVE'S EMBRACE"

There is a question that lingers in my soul
Where do broken hearts go? Do they find solace there?
A journey begins, seeking a path to redemption,
To mend the pieces, to escape from this affliction,
Can they find their way back, to the familiar embrace,
Of open arms waiting, showering love and grace?

In the realm of love, where emotions intertwine,
A flame once ignited, can it never decline?
If somebody loves you, won't they be true?
Looking into your eyes, the answer comes into view.
They yearn for healing, seeking refuge in a love that's revealing,
In those tender moments, when care transcends,
A bond that endures, a love that mends.

For in your eyes, I see the flame still burning,
The love that's unyielding, forever returning,
Through the trials and storms, you still remain,
Caring for me, even though the deepest pain.
So let us not dwell on the where or the how,
But focus on the love that resides in us now,

For broken hearts may wander, but they find their way,
Back to the arms that cherish, come what may.
In this journey called life, where uncertainty roams,
Love's beacon shines bright, guiding broken hearts home,
And if somebody loves you, they'll always be there,
In their eyes, you'll find comfort, love beyond compare.

A JOURNEY WITH GOD BY OUR SIDE

The weight of burdens seemed too much to bear,
In search of healing, they turned to prayer.
Oh, can you heal me, dear Lord above?
For I am lost, in need of your love.
I cannot do this journey alone,
I surrender my troubles, to you I'm prone.
Belief is powerful, a guiding light,
With faith, we can conquer the darkest night.
So, stand up, somebody, speak with conviction,
Lift your hands and join the benediction.

To the King of Glory, we lift our praise,
For His love is mighty in all of our ways.
Do you know Jesus? Hold up your hand,
And let His grace and mercy fill the land.

Oh yeah, yeah, let these words resound,
As we gather, united, standing on holy ground.
Together we find strength, hope, and grace,
As we journey through life, hand in hand, embracing the embrace.
So let us say, yeah, with joyful hearts,
For in His presence, our troubles depart.
In this conversation, hope takes flight,
With a friendly Friend guiding us through the night.

"A JOURNEY OF TRIUMPH"

The realm of mirrors, a reflection is shown,
Revealing the struggles that I've always known.
Body shaming whispers, a cruel, haunting chant,
But remember, my dear soul, you're more than an enchant.

Like a copy and paste, resemblances arise,
Echoes of my mother, both in form and guise.
But know, I am uniquely true,
An individual, with a spirit that shines through.

My siblings, they mirror, my actions they trace,
But their journey's not mines, each walks a separate pace.
It's hard to be loved and understood, it's true,
But within my own heart, acceptance starts anew.

Depression, it lingers, but its grip may now wane,
A glimmer of solace in the midst of the pain,
I've walked through the darkness, emerged to the light,
And found strength in myself shining ever so bright.

Once in the streets, a life fraught with despair,
Gang banging and drugs, a path leading nowhere,
But I rose above, earned an education's crown,
Showing the world that redemption can be found.
DHS, a system that intervened,
Took me from your parents, a family once seen,
But in this new chapter, I've learned to embrace,

The bonds that were formed, as love took their place.

Living without a father, a void that persists,
Yet within my own strength, resilience exists.
For fathers come in many forms, you see,
And love can bloom in the most unexpected decree.

DHS took my kids, a pain hard to bear,
But remember, dear heart, love is always there.
In time, obstacles soften, wounds start to heal,
And the bond between hearts, time cannot steal.

So, in the realm of mirrors, remember this truth,
I am remarkable, resilient, and so full of youth.
Though life may throw chaos, tests and strife,
I'll find my way back to a beautiful life.

©Oceania Smith

A PROMISE FOR LIFE

Within your life, my friend so dear,
I offer solace, wiping away every tear.
In your life, I promise not to harm,
For love and kindness are my charm.
Together we'll navigate this vast expanse,
Facing trials with resilience and a graceful dance.

No matter what others may say or do,
In your life, I'll always stay true.
With each passing day, my love will grow,
A steady flame that will forever glow.
In your life, you're cherished and adored,
A precious soul, let your spirit soar.
I'm here to guide, to lend a helping hand,
In your life, let joy and peace expand.

So, fear not, dear one, for I'll always be nearby,
Through every triumph and every fear.
In your life, know that you're never alone,
Together we'll create a happiness unknown.
Let these words be a gift, a sweet refrain,
In your life, may love always remain.
Forever intertwined, like a melody's embrace,
In your life, may serenity find its place.

STRENGTH UNVIELED

In times of darkness, when hope seems lost,
I found the that came at a cost.
Through sleepless nights and endless strife,
I discovered the power within my life.
There were moments when I couldn't see,
How I would overcome and truly be free.

But with each stumble and every fall,
I rose again, standing proud and tall.
My spirit soared, fueled by faith,
Guiding me through every challenging wraith.
I held my head high, refusing to bow,
For I was not meant to break, I know.

With determination as my shield,
I faced every battle that life revealed.
And though the world may try to break me,
I stood firm, unyielding, and ready.

No, I didn't know my own strength,
But I discovered it at length.
For within me lies a power untold,
A resilience that cannot be controlled.

So let this be a reminder to all,
That even in the face of a daunting wall,
We have the strength to rise above,
To conquer all obstacles with unwavering love.

GUARDIAN OF LOVE

In the depths of sorrow, we gather here,
To honor a father, we hold dear.
His love for us was strong and true,
Now in our hearts, his memory we'll pursue.

He cared for us with every breath,
Guiding us through life's uncertain depths.
His laughter filled our days with joy,
A constant presence we'll forever enjoy.

Though he may no longer walk this earth,
His spirit lives on, a beacon of worth.
In the laughter of grandchildren, his love will reside,
As they grow and flourish, his legacy won't hide.
God called him home, to a place divine,
Where endless love and peace intertwine.

A guardian angel watching from above,
Guiding us gently with everlasting love.
Now we must face each passing day,
Through tears and fond memories, we'll find our way.

For your father's love, it will never cease,
May his soul rest in eternal peace.
In moments of darkness, may you find light,
Knowing that his love will forever shine bright.
Hold onto the memories, let them be your guide,
For in your heart, his love will always reside.

OH, HOW I REGRET

I feel the pain,
Of a love that caused regret to remain.
I loved him so deeply, with all that I had,
But now, in regret, my heart is left sad.

Oh, how I wish I could turn back the time,
And unweave the threads of love's fragile rhyme.
For he, who once brought happiness and cheer,
Now leaves me regretting, shedding a tear.

In his embrace, my joy knew no bounds,
But now I'm left with sorrow that resounds.
The love we shared, like a fleeting flame,
Has left me with regrets I can't reclaim.

Oh, the trust I placed so gently in his hands,
Now shattered like shards in shifting sands.
I long for the days when love felt secure,
But now, my heart's anguish is hard to endure.

Regret lingers, like a bittersweet song,
Reminding me of how we went so wrong.
I yearn to undo the pain that I feel,
But alas, the wounds are too deep to heal.
I regret the moments when I let him in,
When I believed his promises, his every whim.

I regret being blind to his deceptive ways,
And the toll that it took on my yesterdays.

But amidst the regrets, a lesson resides,
To guard my heart and take love in strides.
For even though love may bring pain and strife,
I'll learn from regret and rebuild my life.

So, I'll embrace the lessons that I have learned,
And let the fire of regret be overturned.
For I am stronger, despite the love I've lost,
And wiser for the battles that have crossed.

Regret may linger, but it won't define,
The love and resilience that will intertwine.
I'll cherish the memories, both good and bad,
And find solace in knowing, I'm no longer his "girl" to be had.

SLEEPLESS NIGHTS

In the depths of the night, when shadows loom,
With tear-stained cheeks, I face my gloom.
Sleepless nights plagued by haunting dreams,
Where demons dance, hiding their wicked schemes.

My past weighs heavy, a burden to bear,
Exes' ghosts haunt, leaving heartache and despair.
I long to find solace, to break free from this strife,
But fear grips me tightly, stealing hope from my life.

Scared to rise, afraid to face the day,
My spirit trembles, lost in disarray.
I yearn for release, to let go of this pain,
But darkness surrounds me, driving me insane.

In desperation, I seek solace in dreams,
Hoping someone out there understands my screams.
Wishing upon stars for my dreams to come true,
Seeking refuge from this anguish that I've been through.

Medications prescribed to numb the ache,
But they can't mend the wounds, the memories they make.
The temptation lingers, to overdose and fade,
But deep down inside, a glimmer of hope is laid.
For in these darkest moments, strength will arise,
To lift me from despair and whisk away the lies.

Though the road is tough, and the journey unknown,
I'll find my way back, where self-love is shown.

So as the night fades, and dawn paints the sky,
I'll gather the fragments and learn how to fly.
No longer held hostage by demons in the night,
I'll reclaim my spirit, embrace the morning light.

©Oceania Smith

A WOMAN'S WORTHS

In this world that's sometimes unkind,
Where hearts are broken, dreams confined,
I want to remind young women and girls,
To hold their heads high, let their spirits unfurl.

Don't let men do you wrong, my friend,
For you are destined for greatness, there's no end.
You've overcome struggles, held on so long,
You're standing strong, your spirit so strong.

When your heart was shattered, backstabbed and hurt,
Know that it's okay, embrace yourself, don't desert.
Men may body shame, but it's their insecurity,
Stay confident, love yourself with pure sincerity.

People may lie, wearing masks upon their face,
But your truth will shine through, leaving no trace.
Women may lose loved ones along their journey,
But it's okay, for you'll always carry their memory.

As friendships fade and goodbyes are said,
Remember it is okay, new connections lie ahead.
And if you seek solace in big words, my dear,
Express the depths of your soul without fear.

You are brilliant, capable, and full of grace,
With strength that can withstand any challenge you face.
Keep your heads up, young women, never forget,
You're destined for greatness, don't give up yet.

Believe in yourself, reach for the stars above,
Embrace your worth, spread your wings, and love.
For you are the future, the light shining through,
Young women and girls, the world needs you.

©Oceania Smith

COLD HEARTED LOVE

In a world so cold, my dear, your heart was shattered,
By a love that consumed you, left you feeling battered.
You loved him with all you might, to the very brim,
But in return, his actions were far from grim.

Betrayal and lies, like knives through your soul,
Backstabbing and hurt became your daily toll.
Yet through it all, you stood strong, 19 years and counting,
DHS and Depression, their weight so astounding.

But just when darkness seemed to engulf your way,
Your real family emerged, guiding you through the fray.
They offered a light, a beacon in the night,
Reminding you that love can still shine bright.

Oh, the world we live in, filled with violence and strife,
Where people shoot each other, taking innocent lives.
Young kids dying, bullied, trapped in poverty's grip,
A reality we must face, where compassion must equip.

And amidst this chaos, you long for that dear someone,
The one who had your back, through all you've overcome.
Together you faced thick and thin, hand in hand,
A bond unbreakable, a pillar that'll forever stand.
So, as you rise towards the top, on your journey to success,
Remember the lessons learned, the pain you have redress.

Hold onto the love that remains, for it is your strength,
Embrace the warmth of family, go to any length.

For in this poem, dear human, I hope you can find,
That even in heartbreak, love and hope intertwine.
You are resilient, courageous, and never alone,
With a future brighter than any heartbreak you've known.

©Oceania Smith

LIFE LESSON

In the depths of despair, I once did reside,
On cold city streets where hope seemed to hide.
I worked tirelessly, with every ounce of might,
To escape the darkness and emerge into light.

From stealing this to survive each passing day,
I fought against odds, refusing to sway.
For money can corrupt, it poisons the soul,
Blinding those who let possessions take control.

But I, dear friend, found solace in the truth,
That materialistic things hold no eternal youth.
For what good is wealth if kindness is lost,
When gratitude falters and compassion is tossed?

God, in all His wisdom, can strip us of all,
A humbling reminder, as we stumble and fall.
He can take back it all, the riches and fame,
To teach us a lesson and realign our aim.

So let us not forget our humble beginnings,
The hardships endured, the battles we're winning.
For within our hearts lie stories untold,
Of resilience and strength, as our journeys unfold.
No matter how far we may have come,
Remembering where we're from keeps us humbly strong.
In this tale of redemption, let's never lose sight,

That it's the fire within, that truly ignites.

So, hold your head high, my dear, and don't be afraid,
To embrace your past, where foundations were laid.
For it's in our struggles, we discover our worth,
And the true measure of a soul's rebirth.

As you continue your path, let these words be your guide,
To never let money or possessions divide.
Stay rooted in love, for it will set you free,
To cherish what matters, in this life's symphony.

©Oceania Smith

HER HEART

In the depths of her being, a beating drum,
Lies the essence of her, her heart, so young.
A vessel of emotions, both tender and fierce,
It dances to life's rhythm, never to be coerced.

With each thump and flutter, a tale is told,
Of love and laughter, of stories untold.
Her heart sings melodies of joy and delight,
Guiding her through darkness, like a guiding light.

In times of sorrow, it weeps soft tears,
Cleansing her soul from all her fears.
But it's in the moments of deep connection,
That her heart finds solace, true affection.

Her heart, a canvas for love's masterpiece,
A sanctuary of dreams, a place of peace.
It paints

HEART BREAKER

In the shadows of heartbreak's gloom,
Her soul finds solace, healing wounds.
A symphony of emotions, it weaves,
In the tapestry of dreams, she believes.
Once vibrant and full of life's zest,
She now walks a path that feels distressed.

But within her soul, a strength resides,
To mend the pieces, where love subsides.
Whispers of past echoes, hauntingly nearby,
Yet hope ignites, banishing all fear.
Her soul, a sanctuary, holds the key,
To unlock the door, set her spirit free.

With every tear shed, a phoenix will rise,
From heartbreak's ashes, it seeks to reprise.
For in her soul, resilience takes hold,
Transforming pain into stories untold.

And as time passes, wounds slowly mend,
Her soul learns to love, again ascend.
For heartbreak may leave scars that remain,
But her soul's resilience will never wane.
So let her heartbreak be a bittersweet guide,
A reminder that she's beautifully alive.
In the depths of her soul, a tale is told,
Of strength, of growth, of a love that unfolds.

LETTER TO MY FATHER

In shadows cast by years long gone,
A tale of absence, a mournful song,
A father's love, a child's yearning,
In words unspoken, hearts left burning.

Nineteen years, oh, they slip away,
Still, memories cling, forever they stay,
A bond unseen, a touch untold,
Yet, within your heart, his presence unfolds.

How he never held you, kissed your tears,
Or whispered solace to allay your fears,
Locked away, his voice a distant dream,
But in your heart, his love does gleam.

In the depths of darkness, you grow,
A seed of strength, a love that flows,
A baby girl, born into this strife,
Yet carrying his spirit, a spark of life.

You long to dance in his warm embrace,
To run to him, seeking solace and grace,
To speak your truth, share your joys and fears,
To feel his love, to wipe away your tears.
Oh, the ache within your soul, it burns,
As night descends, and your heart yearns,

The tears that stain your pillow, so cold,
Yet his memory, forever bold.

For on that day, October's embrace,
Nineteen years, a bittersweet space,
You grew up missing him, it's true,
But his love, his essence, forever with you.

Through the trials of this relentless world,
His legacy, in you, is unfurled,
A daughter's love, unyielding and strong,
In this cold, you'll remember, and carry on.

So, sleep, my dear, though tears may fall,
Know that you're cherished, through it all,
For fathers locked away, they still reside,
In hearts of daughters, their love abides.

And as you journey through life's unknown,
Know that his love will forever be shown,
In every beat of your heart, his presence will be,
A testament to love, in eternity.

HIS FIRST BORN

In the depths of longing, a heart confined,
A daughter's sorrow, aching, intertwined,
Locked away, your father, absent and far,
October's anniversary, marking the scar.

Nineteen years, oh, how they swiftly passed,
Leaving behind a void, a love unsurpassed,
Yearning to hug him, to feel his embrace,
To kiss away tears, in this cold, lonesome space.

In this harsh, bitter world, you stand alone,
Without his guidance, your heart feels thrown,
Yearning to run to him, seek his sheltering wing,
To share your burdens, the melodies you sing.

Thoughts of him consume your mind, night and day,
His absence casting shadows, in every way,
Never having hugged him, danced in his arms,
A profound sadness, a life full of qualms.

Oh, how heavy is the weight upon your chest,
A longing unfulfilled, a soul distressed,
But remember, dear one, within this strife,
You carry his spirit, his love, for life.
Though he may be locked within those prison walls,
His love transcends, for it never stalls,

In the corners of your heart, his presence resides,
A beacon of love that forever guides.

Through the sadness, you find strength to endure,
To navigate this world, uncertain and obscure,
For within you lie a resilience so rare,
A daughter's love, an unyielding affair.

On this anniversary, as the years unfold,
May your heart find solace, may it be consoled,
For a daughter's love, it knows no end,
Though apart, your love will always transcend.

So, my dear, hold on to the love you possess,
Embrace the memories, cherish and caress,
For even in the cold, you're not alone,
Your father's love, a warmth forever known.

MOTHERLESS LOVE

In the absence of a mother's embrace,
A different kind of love finds its place.
It's a love that lingers, soft and true,
From those who stand by, supporting you.

The tender touch of a guiding hand,
From father or friend, they understand.
They fill the void with warmth and care,
Showing love that's beyond compare.

Siblings bond tight, like branches on a tree,
Together they weather life's stormy sea.
Their love grows fierce, their hearts entwined,
Through laughter, tears, and every kind.

A motherless love may have a different face,
But it's endless, unwavering in its grace.
For in each heart, a seed is sown,
To nurture and love, to call your own.
So let us cherish this unique love,
Sent from above, a gift from the stars above.
For in its strength, we'll surely find,
A love that's boundless, one of a kind.

DESERVE

Maybe I deserve a chance to speak,
To let my voice be heard, to feel less weak,
Been through struggles, faced my demons too,
But I'm still standing tall, I'm telling you.

I've made mistakes, yeah, I'm not perfect,
But I've learned and grown, I've earned respect,
Been knocked down, but I always rise,
I've seen the lows, now it's time to reach the skies.

Maybe I deserve a shot, to prove my worth,
To show the world what I can bring, my own rebirth,
I've fought my battles, I've paid my dues,
Maybe I deserve a chance to choose.

I've faced judgment, been misunderstood,
But I won't let that define me, knock on wood,
I've got dreams, ambitions in my heart,
And I won't let anyone tear them apart.

I've been through pain, felt the sting of defeat,
But I'm ready to rise, stand on my own two feet,
I've got the fire inside, burning bright,
Maybe I deserve a chance to ignite

I've got a story to tell, a voice to be heard,

I've got passion and determination, that's my word,
I've been knocked down, but I won't stay down,
I'll prove my worth, turn my life around.

(Chorus)
Maybe I deserve a shot, to prove my worth,
To show the world what I can bring, my own rebirth,
I've fought my battles, I've paid my dues,
Maybe I deserve a chance to choose.

(Outro)
So, hear me now, I won't be denied,
I'll keep pushing forward, with my head held high,
I'll make my mark, leave a legacy,
Because maybe, just maybe, I deserve to be free.

RISE AND SHINE

In the morning's gentle embrace,
I sat outside, finding solace in space,
With my loyal cat by my side,
Reflecting on storms I had once defied.
Thoughts of my past, they drifted by,
Of a love lost, a heartfelt sigh,
Yearning for what could not be,
Hoping for a chance to set it free.

But as the sun's rays gently kissed my face,
I felt a warmth that time couldn't erase,
A glow of confidence, a queenly gleam,
Embracing my melanin, a radiant dream.

The future beckoned with each new morn,
Promising change, a chance to be reborn,
And as the morning sun danced in the sky,
I knew within me; strength would never die.

So, in this moment, I let go of the past,
Knowing my journey would always last,
Every lyric, every verse sung anew,
Carrying the echoes of all I've been through.
For just like the morning sun's brilliant light,
I'll rise, shine, and conquer any fight,
With my cat and memories by my side,
Embracing the storms and the sun's loving guide.

EMBRACING THE UNEXPECTED

A tale of love takes its place.
A friend, they say, she's just a friend,
But doubts and questions start to blend.
A phone call rings at a certain time
Awakening doubts, stirring my mind
"I can't take this no more," I say,
As I gather my things and walk away.
Leaving behind all the pain and strife.

But my heart still remains the same
No longer willing to hear what they say.
But in this moment of strength and grace,
A deeper truth begins to chase. For love is never easy,
It's filled with doubts and lingering fear.

So, I took a breath, before I flee,
And listen closely, let me be.
Sometimes friendships become much more,
And sometimes love knocks on our door.
Open your heart, let go of strife,
Embrace the unexpected, the unknown life.

For in these twists and turns we find,
The beauty of love, the ties that bind.
So, as you bounce away in your life
Remember, love's journey is often bizarre.
Be open to possibilities, my friend,
And may happiness find you in the end.

©Oceania Smith

YEARNING FOR TRUE LOVE

I search for love's embrace,
Seeking someone real, a soul to truly embrace.
Someone worth my time, a love that's pure and true,
A person who sees my flaws, yet loves me through and through.
I yearn for someone who won't try to control,
But lets me be free, as my true self unfolds.

No deception or deceit, just a chance to believe,
In something beautiful, a love that will never leave.

But is that too much to ask, I wonder in despair,
As hope starts to fade, lost in the depths of this cold air.
Searching for love, but finding only empty space,
Is it too much to hope for, to find my rightful place?
I long for an answer, to know I'm not alone,
To find someone who'll love me, flaws and all, as their own.

Imperfections don't matter, perfection is not the key,
Just give me a purpose, a reason to love, and be.

I crave somebody who'll treat me like a treasure,
Not like everybody else, but with a love beyond measure.
All they need to do is love me for who I am,
To see the beauty within, and forever be my biggest fan
Maybe it seems like I'm asking for too much,
But in this world so cold, love is a gentle touch.
So, I'll keep searching, hoping to find my missing piece,
A love that's true and real, a love that will never cease.

©Oceania Smith

LETTER TO MY KUZIN

In the midst of darkness, cousin dear,
Hold your head high, have no fear.
For life's challenges may come your way,
But remember, they won't always stay.
Tough times may linger, but they'll pass,
As you persevere, they won't last.
You are a warrior, strong and brave,
God's guiding light will help you pave.

Though the storm may seem relentless,
Know that love surrounds you, endless.
As your big cousin, I'm here to say,
I'll support you each step of the way.
DHS and schools may bring strife,
But together, we'll conquer this life.
You may feel alone, but don't despair,
My love and care, I freely share.

You're 16, facing battles unseen,
Yet through it all, you remain serene.
Remember, my dear, you're not alone,
With courage and strength, you'll be shown
So, keep pushing, never lose sight,
Your journey will lead to a shining light.
Embrace life's ups and downs with grace,
Good times will soon take their rightful place.
In this poem, I want you to know,
That I love you, dear cousin, so.
No matter what hardships you may face,
I'm here for you, in every embrace.

MY SISTERS KEEPER

In the realm of love, a bond so true,
A tale of sisters, in foster care they grew.
Through the twists and turns, life's intricate maze,
Together they stand, bound in heartfelt ways.

Isabella, with strength and grace she'll bloom,
Her spirit radiates, defeating any gloom.
Regina, a beacon of light in the darkest of nights,
Guiding her sisters with love that ignites.

Janiyah, a fighter with a heart so fierce,
In her presence, the demons will disperse.
Through hurdles and trials, they won't be deterred,
For love and support, their spirits will be stirred.

In this journey of life, they'll never be alone,
For their sisters keep them, firm as a stone.
Wrapped with a love that knows no bounds,
They'll conquer any fear that surrounds.

God watches over, their mama will mend,
With time and healing, their wounds will transcend.
Together they'll flourish, their dreams will come true,
A family, united, where love will imbue.
So, hold on tight, dear sisters of mine,
You're connected, like stars that eternally shine.
Your love and resilience will guide you through,
Trust in the journey, for a brighter tomorrow awaits you.

BABY BROTHER

In a family of love and care,
Jeremiah, my brother, always aware.
With four sisters, he stands tall,
A guardian, keeping us from a fall.

Head held high, pushing through the strife,
A beacon of strength in this challenging life.
For me and mama, he carries the weight,
Upholding our Legacy, both early and late.

As my younger brother, he shines so bright,
Guiding us with his unwavering light.
In this world that can be tough,
Jeremiah, never let it snuff.

For God is with you, by your side,
And through it all, you'll always glide.
DHS may test your resolve,
But don't let them bully, don't let them dissolve.

Stay true to yourself, my black young king,
An inspiration to many, let your spirit sing.
In brotherhood, you stand tall and strong,
A pillar of love, where you belong.
Jeremiah, you are your sisters' protector,
A kinship bond that none can dissect or reject.
Keep your head up, keep pushing through,

For we're here for you, always true.

So, carry on, dear brother, with pride,
Knowing that we're forever by your side.
Together we'll weather any storm that comes,
With love and support, our hearts are drums.

Embrace your role, our brother so dear,
For in unity, our strength shall never veer.
Jeremiah, my brother's keeper, always stand,
A testament to the power of family's hand.

©Oceania Smith

MOTHERS WOMB

In a mother's warm embrace,
A love so pure, a sacred space.
Her arms a haven, her heart a guide,
Through every storm, she'll stand beside.

With tender hands and gentle care,
She nurtures dreams, she's always there.
She'll wipe away tears and heal all pain,
Her love a beacon in life's terrain.

In her eyes, a warmth that never fades,
A love that shines with no barricades.
She sacrifices, she gives her all,
For her children, she'll always stand tall.

Her love knows no bounds, no measure,
A bond that's built to last forever.
She holds the power to mend and heal,
To teach life's lessons, to help us feel.
So let us honor our mothers dear,
Whose love and strength are always near.
For in their love, we find our light,
Guiding us through both day and night.

"URBAN ANXIETY'S CACOPHONY"?

In the city's chaos, a cacophony reigns,
Siren's wail, guns crackle, and fear sustains.
Ambulances rush, fire trucks scream by,
A constant reminder, life can pass us by.

I wonder, will I be the next to fall?
Will death come knocking, hearing sirens call?
Or will my final breath be in a hospital bed?
Fears and worries swirl in my troubled head.

Please, not my family, I beg and pray,
Spare them from harm, let them live another day.
But the storm rages on, a relentless beat,
A symphony of fear, a constant repeat.

Oh, how I yearn for peace, a calm embrace,
Free from the grip of violence, a safe place.
But the alarm rings loud, a warning in my ear,
A reminder that danger lurks, always nearby.

I'm scared to step out, diseases spread,
Viruses claiming lives, young ones falling dead.
Gun violence snatches away, without a care,
Leaving families shattered, with tears to share.

I long to breathe freely, without dread's weight,

To walk the streets, without fear's constant debate.
But the world outside seems to spin out of control,
A never-ending cycle of hurt, and lives stolen whole.

So, I hold on tight, to hope's fragile thread,
Praying for a dawn, when peace will be spread.
When love will conquer fear, and guns will fall still,
And every breath will be a gift, without the chill.

A JOURNEY WITH GOD BY OUR SIDE

The weight of burdens seemed too much to bear,
In search of healing, they turned to prayer.

Oh, can you heal me, dear Lord above?
For I am lost, in need of your love.
I cannot do this journey alone,
I surrender my troubles, to you I'm prone.

Belief is powerful, a guiding light,
With faith, we can conquer the darkest night.
So, stand up, somebody, speak with conviction,
Lift your hands and join the benediction.

To the King of Glory, we lift our praise,
For His love is mighty in all of our ways.
Do you know Jesus? Hold up your hand,
And let His grace and mercy fill the land.

Oh yeah, yeah, let these words resound,
As we gather, united, standing on holy ground.

Together we find strength, hope, and grace,
As we journey through life, hand in hand, embracing the embrace.

So let us say, yeah, with joyful hearts,
For in His presence, our troubles depart.
In this conversation, hope takes flight,
With a friendly Friend guiding us through the night.

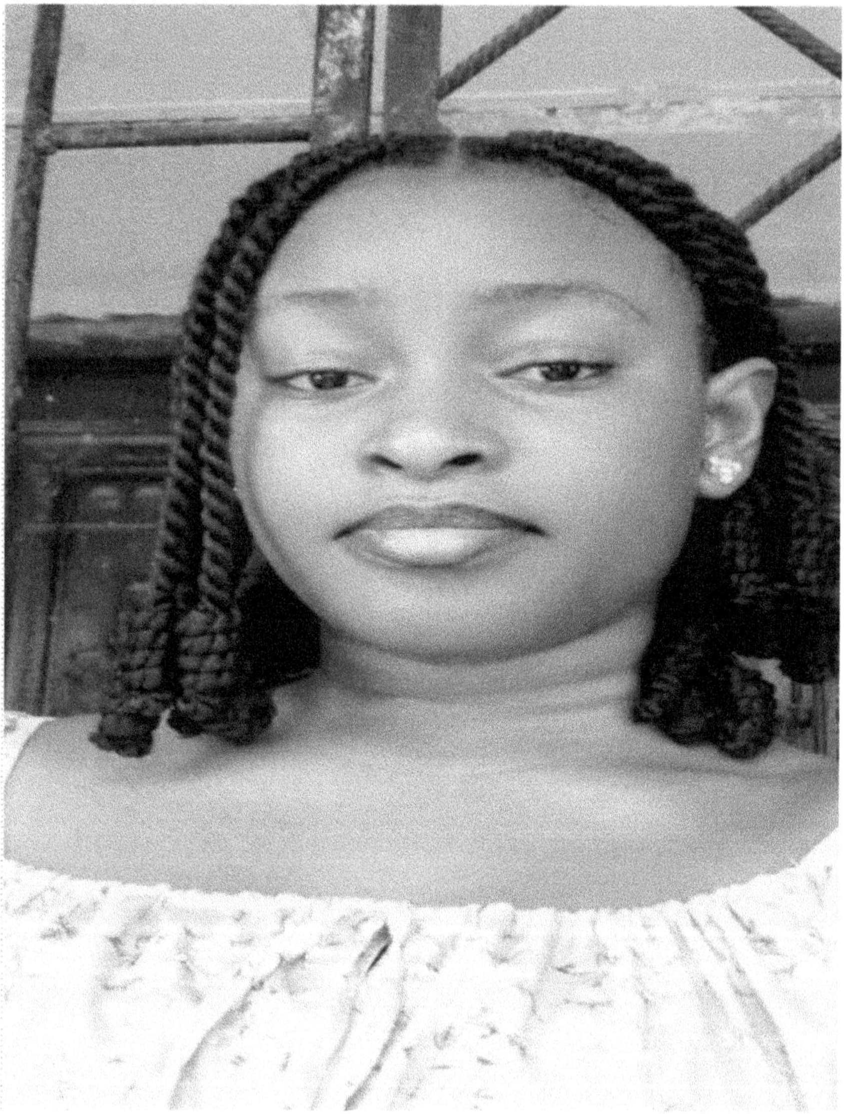

OBIORA PRECIOUS AKACHUKWU

COUNTRY: NIGERIA

WHY DO YOU WRTIE POETRY?

Poems are the easiest way for me to express emotions. I write poems to correct most of the ill miscellaneous social vices in my society. I use poems to convey a clear scripted message.

I write poems to educate and create awareness on some of the ills that plague my society. I'm an advocate for egalitarianism and see both genders as equal. Most of my poems are centered on women, precisely African women finding their purpose.

WHAT IS YOUR MESSAGE TO THE WORLD?

My message to the world is to maintain peace and healthy rivalry between Nations of the world.

Also, to see each other as stairs attaining great heights and contributing to world peace and tranquility.

CHAPTER THIRTEEN
OBIORA PRECIOUS AKACHUKWU

WOULD YOU STILL LOVE ME?

Would you still love me,
If this pretty eye turned blind?
Would you still love me,
if those elegant legs went lame?
Would you still cherish our love,
if I had a tumor and had only two Months to live?
Would you love me,
if this glossy black skin
turned soar and wrinkled with leprosy?
If the love you profess,
is only for the better
and not the worse
then you should leave.
If you're in for the physique
and aesthetics,
you should leave.
I can't waste time
on people not worth the while.
I have a life to live,
a goal to achieve
and dreams to actualize.
You'll have to go through
my worst to get to my good.
Back out while you still can...

LIKE GOD'S ON EARTH

Like gods on earth,
Thuds of their feets
Shake mountains.
A quake is inavertable.
Voice like many oceans put together.
A voice that splits the cedars of Lebanon
And divide fury furnaces.
Like gods on earth
Thy names known in all pillars,
Pillars of the Lord's house.
Making waves in history
And tides in the present.

Like gods on earth
Cruelty is brought to shambles,
Oppression is destroyed.
War will be traded for peace,
Sorrow for Joy
An atmospheric change of favor
And radiating glory.
Like mighty gods on earth
My words are my sword
They don't kill but create.
I am a god.

A LETTER TO MY PEN

It's been long.
It's been a long time I scribbled.
I'm not ignoring you, trust me.
I'm always busy with something,
Ideas come too late or too early.
I had to survive,
So, I had to focus on work.
So sorry it got all my emotion,
All it wanted was my undivided devotion.
But somehow my heart feels
Safer when I scribble.
I'm sorry for how cold you felt,
Missed the warmth you and I shared.
You display my emotions unsaid.

You're my light,
Unveiling me to my limelight.
You did me a favor
By writing this letter addressed to you.
I promise to never ever leave again.

-

AFRICA

The African way,
Our African way.
Our culture, our heritage.

The taut- tat taut-tat,
Sound of the dun-dun drum.

The melodious harmony of the oja.
Aligning sweet music.

The awe shivers of the udu.
Sending shivers down our spines.

The whining waists of our maidens
In collaboration with the sounds of the olopo.

The ujaga following the movements of their feets,
All resulting to a very lovely combination of music.

Ohh!! How I exclaim thy beauty,
How I sing of thy strength and prowess,
Africa, my continent.
My Home.

INGRATITUDE

I trusted you,
But you took my trust and trampled on it.
You gave me hope,
But you disappointed me each time.
I gave you my time,
But it was labelled worthless.

I have nothing else to render.
You painted yourself black
With your very hands.
I've seen that which is the real you.
I need no other confirmation.

I helped you,
But you stabbed me.
I gave you a helping hand
But you stung it with your viciousness.

I'm not a judge,
But with a layman's observation,
You're an ingrate.

COURAGE

The courage to change
I have a purpose
To summon the rendezvous of the needy
But feels like I'm alone in all this
I need that voice, that'll say
"You're not alone in all this"
"Together we can do all these things"
I'm stuck in the weeds.

Dear God…
I'm taking the courage to change.
I want to heal.
I agree not to be bittered,
So that my life can matter.
I'll keep my face towards the sunshine
So that the shadows will fall behind me.
I can't expire without giving out all I got.

I'm the water to the thirsty,
The food to the famished.
The oil to dry destinies.
I want to make them better.
I want them to see the real me,
Filled with the love inside.
I'll pick up their broken pieces,
And make them feel the peace.
I want to heal them better,

Better than the abandoned minds of Delhi…

What the word I,
Would love to accomplish,
Are more than the stars in our Galaxy.
Dear God…
The courage to change.

TALKING BONES

I'm scared!!
I heard a screeching noise,
A noise from my insides

I heard a voice
"I am the femur,
I balance the hip bone
And the patella.
I am a very important bone in the body.
So, I deserve to be the head".

The metacarpals cut in
"You can hold nothing
Without my help.
You can only work with
Your hands because I let you do so.
Only I deserve to be the leader".

I was dumbfounded.
Were my bones really talking??
I could really hear them speak
They were arguing amongst themselves

Then the cranium spoke,
"My importance cannot be over emphasized.
I protect the brain from harm.
Without me there will be disorder in the body.
I am the one true ruler".

The atlas and axis chips in,
"You need a head in the body, right?
I make the head upright.
Without me the head will never
Stand, nod or turn.
If I can control the direction of the head,
Only I should be the leader ".
The noise was becoming louder
Each bone wanted to disengage
From my body.
I was scared.
I didn't want to die.

Then I heard a voice,
It spoke with finality and authority.
It was the rib cage
"I protect the heart, lungs, liver
And partly protects the kidney.
I protect the vital organs of the body
But yet I didn't boast of it.
Without my existence,
No one will thrive
But irrespective of that,
I still see equal importance in us.
We cannot do without each other.
We all make up the skeletal system
Divided we fall, United we stand".

DANVERS

Thank you for coming into my life,
I once experienced dark and gloomy days
But you came into my life
And brightened my world.

Your great support is my strongest pillar.
You make me see things positively,
You helped change this pessimistic aspect of my thinking.
You made me see more essence in life.
Thanks for always standing by me.

Your kind and true nature
Can't be compared to another.
Your words are ever soothing,
Calming the fiercest of nerves.
You turned this guttural atmosphere,
To the best I never imagined.
Your caring attitude so lovely and tender,
Soothes my skin like that of a new born.

You're one of the finest men,
Fine in attitude, bold in carriage.
Lovely in character, one of the rarest.
You move with a peaceful aura.
You've proved that they are still good men on earth.

OLAEDO

Elders,
Have you seen what has become of our daughter?
Olaedo is now the star fruit everyone wants to taste.
She parades the community exposing her big breasted chest.

Her father, Chief Mbakwe's death,
Unlocked her waywardness.
As soon as Chief Mbakwe was laid to rest,
The chains that made her chaste was buried alongside with him.
Now she sleeps with men,
Both young and old
For the benefits of a basket of dried fish.

Elders would you Condon this rash behavior??
Shouldn't she be banished?
She's a plague on the fine men of our society.
She has reduced men of valor to waste with her beauty.

Even His royal majesty, Igwe Agwu is under her influence.
Olaedo waits under the odan tree in broad daylight,
She waits for men she could trap
With her wanton lies and fictious tongue.
Something has to be done
Before she grows mightier than her superiors.

OBOSHI

Have you all heard??
That oboshi, the god's of the river Oloshi,
Has devoured one of our maidens.
It has continually swallowed our men and women.
An appeasement must be made,
To escape its voluminous wrath.

An oracle was consulted and
This time around,
It doesn't want cow heads
As it has always requested.
It wants the innocent blood
Of our virgins.
Ohh!! What has befallen our community?...

Shall we give up our daughters this time??
Shall we sit back and watch as the heads of our sisters and children are ripped off their bodies??
Ohh!
What painful tumult in our own fatherland?
Is there any way to escape this impending doom on our land??

MY SUPERMAN

My superman
A pillar of support,
Present in the darkest days
And brightest nights.
In the sunshine and the rain,
He's always there to guide me.
He has always been ever present in my life.

My super Hero,
A rare specie of Homo Sapien.
He is love and care personified.
He said, "I'll always be there,
No matter the phase of life you maybe on"
I can't thank you enough,
Cause you're a man of your word.

My super model,
He was present,
When momma birth me.
My first love, my darling Daddy.
How could I not return this love??
When males are hustling for their moms,
I'll hustle for you.

You're very much appreciated dad.
My super mentor,
I appreciate your efforts
By each passing nanosecond.
You contributed in making me a star
And I'll make you pass its limits…

THIS DAY ROUTINE

Every Sunday ritual,
Looking weary as usual,
All because I want to be punctual,
I attend service with my unsatisfied belly.

I am famished and ravenous,
Praising God with a rumbling tummy.
An unending war of worms eating my walls.
But I know by dusk,
I'd be filled to my heart's content
Filled from the rich soil of my abode
AFRICA.

AN ODE TO MY MOTHER

As I gaze at the qualities
Of this wonderful creature,
I'm left amazed.
Her glossy black skin,
Her beautiful eyes like stars of a night.
She takes graceful steps
Like that of a gazelle.
I eulogize your aesthetic qualities
By each passing nanosecond.
Out of her firm fleshed ripe fruit
Flows milk and honey.
Her words, ever soothing
Calming the fiercest of nerves.
What marvels me more,
Is her sky rocketing perseverance.
Her endurance is overwhelming.
She's the house minder, a wife
A mother and at times a father.
She's a good listener.
My personal adviser.
She might not be able
To do great things,
But she can definitely do small things
In a great way.
I love and will always love you mom.

SLAVERY AND UNITY

Chains of servitude,
Cuffed round their productive hands.
Slavery cuffed the ankles of their souls.
Dereliction decapitated the epics of their lives.

Heart flashes into the stories
Of the wise sage.
When the ancient Africans
Were sold into slavery.
The stuttering lips of my pen
And the screeching noise it utters,
Can't show the tones of pain within.
The thought of how Africans were marginalized
brings a raging scenario of pain.

Enough of the pains,
Let's gather the gains.
Let's forget the scars inflicted on us.
Together we can give meaning to
an epoch lost in antiquity.
Africa is our heritage
A home that embraces our color.
Africa our roots, our origin.
Let's welcome unity
For we are one.

COLLIDING FORCES

My lovely smile covers
The broken pieces within.
Self-reassurances still hopes on hope.
My enduring strength in my weaknesses.
My gains in my pains.
I'm the toughest I ever heard or known of.
I've tasted not just the tip,
But down to the base of an iceberg.

Just base in the eastern heart of our land,
But my mind's far west.
Essence beckons on the meaningfulness in me to awake.
The voice says,
"Live and let live".

NIGERIA

Nigeria, my country,
Where sunshine and laughter never seem to end.
A place of warmth and vibrant cheer,
Hospitality is our virtue.

With open arms, Nigeria greets us all,
Inviting us to answer its gentle call.
The call for the compatriots.
A symphony of colors fills the air,
As nature blooms with utmost flair.

The days stretch out in golden hue,
Inviting adventures, both old and new.
From sandy shores to mountain peaks,
Nigeria whispers secrets that our heart seeks.

The sun dances upon the glistening sea,
As waves caress the shore with glee.
In my country's embrace, we find solace deep,
A chance to unwind, to dream, to leap.

The melody of laughter fills the breeze,
As joyful picnics and barbecues please.
Families gather, hearts intertwine,
In my country's embrace, love truly shines.
Fireworks illuminate the velvet sky,
A dazzling display, painting dreams up high.

Nigeria ignites the spark of freedom's flame,
As we celebrate with pride, our nation's name.

So let us be proud Nigerians with open hearts,
Embracing its blessings, its vibrant arts.
May this country be filled with joy untold,
As we journey together, bold and bold.
Be Nigerians, with all your splendor,
A better chapter, a story to remember.
In your embrace, we find hope anew,
As we bid farewell to the past and start anew.

THE WELLS' DIGGER

"Hayaya Heyaya"
Judgement has been passed.
Emeka the well digger
Has been sentenced to death.
He dug on one of kings' fertile lands.
Emeka eme la ihe o jiri nwuru Emeka!
The only son of his father,
Will soon be beheaded.

He was every maiden's trophy boy.
Lustfully captivating them with his smile,
Throwing charming winks
At every maiden he crossed paths with.
Drowning himself in every ocean he came across.

Unfortunately for him,
His escapades with the princess,
Was the last straw.
He touched the tail of a lion.

The king was so dismayed,
His apple is preggies
With the child of a pauper.

Emeka lowers his head in shame.
He was the man who won laurels
For digging wells
Now he has been devoured by one.
Only if he could control his hood,
Then this shouldn't have transpired...

KARMA

Don't talk.

But speak.

Don't just speak,

Speak with evidence.

Not only evidence,

But with courage

And an armor of backings.

Hey you!

Yes you!

Don't trample over people.

Watch your back,

They're coming for you.

Karma is everything.

Karma is a relaxing thought.

Karma is the ticking hand of a clock.

KARMA IS KARMA!

ABIGIRL PHIRI

COUNTRY: ZIMBABWE

WHY DO YOU WRITE POETRY?

I write poetry because it gives me the authority to tackle anything and everything regarding topical issues that we face on a day-to-day basis. In addition, poetry gives me solace in my times of need.

WHAT IS YOUR MESSAGE TO THE WORLD?

My message for the world is for it to unify as individuals, treat each other kindly. This is because it is the ecclesiastic thing to do, being your brother's or sister's keeper.

CHAPTER FOURTEEN
ABIGIRL PHIRI

UNDERAGE FOR THE MARRIAGE BED

Can't believe the injustice
Introducing me to carnal relations
Without so much as a thought
To my shocking tender age Just about yesterday

12-year-old Nancy expired
Succumbing to her internal bleeding
Gone too soon A life wasted away
Hell bent on pleasing a pedophile

Thriving on manipulating the youngsters
Too afraid to marry his own age, childish
Cradle snatcher Peddling falsehood of doctrines
Hiding behind the curtain of unreligious norms
Supported by premedieval cultural beliefs
The young dead girls moan from the dead
Failed by uncaring authorities

Deprived by the social fabric
To uplift the girl child Condemned to a half marriage
Sanctified by false prophets
Ululated by wicked cougar mothers
Certifying marriage of conveniences
Age factor carefully avoided
Throwing education's wisdom in the bin
Pushed in the motherhood clutches
Before her young womb can carry a seed
Shame on inhuman behavioral tendencies.

HAD I KNOWN?

If wishes were horses Beggars would ride
Galloping freely in the wind
The horse already out of the barn
Headed for a new journey
Leaving behind both baggage and family
Reuniting with the maker
Waiting patiently to eternally accommodate
Permanent tenants in at first, foreign land
With the passage of time realizing
This is the final resting place
Talked by the great prophets in another life
The interchanging of life's planes
Complex to comprehend but the end being the same
Welcomed in the tight circle
Of family long gone Blood is thicker than water
Even in this new beginning You blend in with your own
Forgetting the momentary shock
Accepting the end of each story Had you known?
You could have left with a kind word

Dried their tears with assurance
That in this new space You are free as a bird
With time, all will be reunited
The epiphany of life.

MUSIC TO MY EARS

The language of poets
That flows smooth sailingly
Rolls on their hypnotizing tongues
Enshrouded in intimacy
Present since the age of time
Overcoming obstacles
Superseding triumph
Comforted in the warm embrace
A lover proffering unconditional love
Showered with kisses
Divorced from deceit
Enchanted with the safe haven of ownership
The beautiful tug of war
Being owned and to own
Transcending to after life
Where still,
Your kisses are free of malice
Love that has no borders
Mutual feelings respecting
The difference of colors
Ignited by our heated loins
Procreation is the final decision
Standard procedure dictating
Love and only true love
Is music to the ears.

THE LITTLE BOOK

The passport of life's poetry
Aiding you in your foot loose travels
Border jumping life hurdles
To a land full of greener pastures
Brother and sisters made into one
Through the connectivity of a visa
Boundaries dealt away with
Speaking in one common language
The gospel being of peace living
Flourishing and nourishing in host countries
Never losing your novel identity
Importantly acquiring different culture tastes
Where life sends you
The winds blow in companion
Directing you in that same direction
The compasses 4-sided ultimatum
Seeing you in the safe haven of words

LADIES FIRST

For so long she has been silent
Not sure how to maneuver
In the odyssey of life
Filled with random thoughts
Unsure how to put them across
Finding her voice
The liberating feeling of freedom
To express herself freely
Clearly free from self-consciousness
Able to clear her tight throat to speak
Like a caged bird set free
Assuredly she wears a big smile
Big enough, to accommodate all
Running and laughing in the wind
Twin rivers of mirth run her ruddy cheeks
Ladies first now a broken record
Times have changed
The unprecedented birth of gentlemen
Side by side with her polar opposite
Together they are Adam's progenies

WHEN THE UNIVERSE CHOOSE YOU

The hands of time
Works according to their chime
Specifically at the clock's prime
No one can tell
Only the universe holds the spell
For one to come out from the shell
When it ticks
The fetus in the womb kicks
That's how the universe picks
The universe always has its take
Followed by the rewarding perks
It can break you but mostly it makes

FINALLY

Marshall saw it all, So sad
An old man Having no family
Finally, Marshal said
All hands on this mission
Giving companionship
Amusing him Daily
Happily, Half a loaf
Would go a long way
Then doing nothing
Sadly, All in all Old man
Talking and laughing
Drunk God took him

Finally, Marshal was sad
Finding companionship was hard
That's how it is Painful Accordingly
Marshal was now mindful
Days on Sadly, Marshal was going
Out of town to start his solo taught craft
Motivation Sad lad's Bad individuals
Starting from scratch old days
Worth to stay in the past
As Marshal Took to his calling
Motivational coach on a mission
To call This world his rightful lair
Soon, his son Was born

And Marshal thought About his prodigy
Boy this son, Junior Alan Not Aladin
Which Mary thought
But junior champ Alan was forward
Just as past had it old man's soul
Had finally Found Junior Alan
As a host Born again
With Marshal Finally.

THE USELESS WARNING

First, l sneezed really hard
I was never best friends
With offensive smells Smoke topped the list
Opening my sleep clad eyes,
I was met with the licks of flames
So huge, like Moses with the burning bush
Instead, this was my inherited house
Secondly, l panicked Lost at ends, how to escape
The alarm had not sounded off
That was odd, for l could have heard it
Pulling on my discarded silky nightie
This had been a busy night
Before Ben left for his house
The advantage of having your

boyfriend just next door
Thirdly, choosing options really quick
Discarding the least attractive
I pulled on my Wonder woman boots
It was now or never
My only regret, having
not had time to eat my cake
As the door was engulfed in flames
The window beckoned safety
I was going to lose everything
The only thing leaving intact was my life

I couldn't even say the same
for my badly shaken sanity
Lastly, climbing out through the
tree next to my childhood window
The alarm had the audacity to go off
In tandem with that of the fast approaching,
fire engine red brigade humongous autoboot
Scratches, bruises and first degree burn on my skin
I landed on my feet as a cat Ma'am, are you alright,
the concerned police asked Boom, blast and heck the
house exploded before l replied
Hell, hath no fury like a homeless woman
Left only with the silky nightie on my back

COMING TO TERMS

As the term comes to an end I am coming to terms
I will freely be able to listen to Terms The terms and conditions
Many have a hard time taming
Only sheer grit, driving in highway without turning
Consider this term Without idea terminating
Grasping quickly like Terminator quest to annihilating
At the term, the times of struggles were officially preterm
Extermination would never be able to grace our post terms
Now it's full term the burgeoning stomach whose
occupant flipping books of tram Waits for the resident first ride in the pram,
The terms and conditions are always the same
Black, white, red, colorless We all come to terms of the game Life.

GIRLS THAT WE ARE

As we come into the world Stealing the hearts of many
Pink barbies We have a great mission
Walk on our own two feet Learn from our mistakes
Care for those who need us Angels of empathy
Standing up for ourselves in every space we find ourselves in
Juggling the balls life throw in the end, winning and queening
Misogynists our arch enemies Feminists' doctrines our daily bread
Girl power unifying us all the little girl in every woman clamoring
for identity You and you, are the enlightened girl child

DEAR FUTURE

You, l have always loved, you l have always known

You will be the only last feature standing

Promise me you will go in time

Promise me you will walk down memory lane

Promise me you will talk about me

The legacy that l leave is in writing

The mark that l live is my work

The testament that l was here is my past

Remember 2023

Remember what transpired over the years before 2100

Remember us all the creatives who had hope for the future

Please be kind to my progenies, please be mindful of all my teaching

Please be my advocate for l will be long gone.

WONDERS NEVER CEASE TO END

The identical twins, tax abuse and tax avoidance
Are exacerbating the smuggling of precious stones in abundance
Illicit financial flow is definitely not in cadence
At the expense of both the marginalized people and environment's burden
The natural balance is eroded
The formal nexus between getting a mining concession
and regularly paying tax has been degraded
The beauty of the mining trade has unfortunately faded
The bad guys have seen to that driven by their ambitions so shredded
We cry for what could have been of our economy
Which could have benefitted us all at the corrupts ignominy
Whilst this is mother nature's sodomy
Without doubt, the complicit of the elite and
the porous entry points are the mining's story bigamy.

WIDOW

The eyes are the mirrors of the soul or they are the windows of the soul

Either way those of a widow Are wizened with grief

Weighed down with tears threatening to fall

Bruised beyond measure She is a shell of her former self

With her husband gone she has little to look forward to

What with no children to comfort her

Time and life have been so cruel to snatch her husband

Memories flooding her mind She can't keep up with reality

Wasn't it just yesterday when they got married?

Ferried to that exotic little paradise

Everything just falling in place like a perfect 6 on a rolled dice

Time then seemed to move so fast Tied and joined to the hip

They had the time of their life

This was before the freak accident on the way back

There was so much blood, heck He didn't stand a chance at all

Died at the spot, pall Merciful heavens

Be mindful of the withered widows.

TIK TOK

Tik Tok for some has turned to be a death trap
As the addiction to the views has rendered them useless
With stalkers prowling loose
Whilst nest of vipers in the form of cyber bullying
Daily trade insults, what on earth is going on
Nevertheless, if born to rule the world
Tik Tok is the best talent platform display
Rise up to the occasion
Reach a wide audience, ensnaring your niche
Bonus point, looking like you have stepped out of an advertisement
Tik Tok our latest heartthrob
This new tech app has shaken the ground beneath us
A place not only for the movers and shakers
But for all and sundry to showcase their talents
Sharing good educational content in spades
Everybody please takes a front row seat.

BRING ON YOUR A GAME

Even if beauty and youth fade Still With twinkling eyes

I will be the winner who takes it all Form any opinion about me

Take even an educated guess Still,
I will never fail to raise the bar high

Go along stroking each other's ego
but when l decides to put an appearance

My work will strike too close to home Still,
you will hang over my every word

As l set my foot down Solidifying that l am the "Master"

BROKEN PROMISES

Betrayed by the one you love Bottled emotions and having no one

Not even one person to turn to This turn of events is drastic

Like a criminal who takes the fall out
We have burnt our bridges alright

Once bitten twice shy I cry silently in my heart

Putting on a brave front each morning Only God knows my plight

I have learnt the hard way, Earth to me as my mind keeps reeling

I try to figure out the best plan to err is to be human

But to me, once the trust is gone you have lost me It's
weighing heavily on my conscience

You actually hit a raw nerve Unfortunately,

now l can't even forgive myself.

BUFFET

Eat your heart out Here are loads of delicacies
It's a feast fit for a king Please do eat your fill
Even if you eat like a pig No one will take notice
Enjoying their own food Fill up your plate and dig in
Bon Appetit Cherie Pour the wine to your heart's content
Let's give a toast Bottoms up

WORDS ARE FOR EVER

Reading is our culture Writing is our religion
Poetry our daily devotion Words that won't be easily erased
Words that will live through the end of time
Words that are forever and ever Literature is our sustenance
Creative writing is our pledge Poetry our soul food.

SLEEPLESS NIGHTS

In the dead of the night Tossing and turning
Feeling useless like humpy dumpty
Hearing the rain doing pity patty on the roof
It's tough
Feels like the end of the world, topsy-turvy
But the harsh truth is that it's only an
Up and down scenario
Thinking of the starry night in Rio
When all was roses and wine
Before sleep evaded me and I felt
Wretched like ashes and cloth
Rotting in the night
No longer feeling high and mighty
Like in the day
But loosing focus whilst grumping and rumpling.

HELP!

Please call 91, I need help
My mental health Is in tatters
Tattered gown Shredded memories
Dreading the next day
Forgetting the essence of life
Death seems the best outlet
Please release me Let me go
I need a peace of mind
Contradicting voices in my head
Constantly depressed and sad
This time it is really bad
Bit by bit l am dying inside, dead
Depressed, Hurt Emotionally drained
Somebody lends me a helping hand
Before it is too late to turn back
Welcome to Hades empire

PAMELA ATIENO OMONDI (PAMWRITES)

COUNTRY: KENYA

WHY I WRITE POETRY:

To me Poetry works as a line of alleviation that is within poetry I can easily ease my thoughts, my worries without having to look for someone to talk to, it makes me talk to myself, debate and find a solution, thus I write poetry because it is a field of self-discovery to me, a house of togetherness for all, I am able to share my thoughts with the world and identify with others with the same ideas or situations elsewhere without necessarily coming together to discuss it, thus with poetry I am able to uplift lives, entertain all in their respective ventures in just some few lines of words(short and precise) and provide relief uniquely. I write poetry because it entertains me to communicate big in small portions. I love poetry, I find it in me to write. I remember writing poetry calling it lyrics for songs, I used to sing them instead of reciting and when I matured, I understood I have been in love with poetry all along and so the journey continued till date

MESSAGE TO THE WORLD:

Finding one's passion is key to positive life, invest in your passion, free living, one should not force to fit in a society, one's passion becomes their wealth, we should not aim to live like others but aim to be our own version. To the upcoming writers like me, don't give up, don't aim to get money, find a reason for your writing, communicate and change lives, the work sells and earn on its own.

CHAPTER FIFTEEN
PAMELA ATIENO OMONDI (PAMWRITES)

I HEARD SHE COMMITTED SUICIDE

When she stood, she was shining.
She was that girl, so elegant without flaws.
When she smiled, to you and I, she was okay,
But did we ever think she might be drowning
Or was in an awful state?

Or is it that her smile was enough
That we paid no attention to her at all?
She might have needed to be well, but she couldn't
Because to us she had a smile
Not knowing her pain had taken its roots beneath.

She was dying inside though she smiled.
And now she is at rest because she committed suicide.
The smile that you and I knew faded
Her smile had lifted her burden
And never ask her.

She committed suicide and sadly

She was just human, she might need to cry
A shoulder to lean on, a place to hide
And a life to carry on.
But we," told her "To be perfect, to be smart and so she smiled,

She was tired of smiling while no one asked how she was,
Her world, the smile, had become so painful to live for
Because you and I stood in care of her smile,
When she, silently counted her tears.
Now, I heard she committed suicide, she couldn't smile anymore

She owed her heart a smile, while she gave ours a smile.
If we asked her, she would have had it real,
Yes, we ought to lend her a shoulder, a place to hide
And a hand of direction.

IT SHOULD ALL BE THE DAY TODAY

It should all be the day today When it was all green like yesterday,
Do you get that scary feeling When it shines and takes away your calm?
Do you feel that smell of mud after the rain
That makes you wish to sniff it all?

What about the hilly air that remains in the morning
From the high mountains and green vegetations?

Why then drain that water of the swamp that freshens
The air when the cool wind blows across?
Why build that industry in my space of leafy vegetation
Taking away my source of solace and giving me eardrum breakage?

Why not add me a layer of solace from that mahogany and eucalyptus
That you hungrily peel off to make that groaning house?
Why not add me more baobab to plant and cover it up?
Why not educate that village man to use "dung" instead?

How do you save the high temperatures I feel now
When all you have done is drain, clear and smoke the green ones.
Who will regulate and stand for that swamp, forest if you and I don't?

I stand for it, I tell you, guard your home, reject the pest.
Let you hear the cries that echoes high across the earth.

We cry for justice, awaken the freshness of the air from pollution,
Let us stand, make every step, every action a steer
To conserve, create and clean the mother earth
And make it a home, a harmonious humanity where it was before.

© Pamwrites

GIVE ME ATTENTION, LISTEN TO ME

When I called out no one cared
Because they considered me an outcast.
I cried to be heard,
But my voice echoed back like a fist.
Why am I different?

Why am I too different to make sense?
I felt lonely by myself
With nights shorter and days longer,
Darkness upon the sunrise,
I thought of peace in the air.

I paced hard in my mind and said,
What a better way to feel the peace
To uproot the unwanted
And what to have people think of me?
Ooh, I got it!

A smile amidst unseen pain flows
Maybe I will get the attention
Once I hear no more.
I will have minds under my feet,
What a better way to have a heart's desire!

I thought of having peace
And I found it away between the dark,
With my mind racing hard on.

Decisively, I rest on my chair,
Never to wake up for I found peace

Away from the pretentious of the living.
I now rest within my walls
Where no one lingers but me,
It makes me happy, I rest on

©Pam@writes

IT NOW PINCHES

Back then, I smiled childishly at your words,
It is now that I understand they were sweet nothings,
Then, it felt costly to lose you,
but now it is all cheap to have had you,
It feels so cloudy to think of you, because your presence was
nothing but poison,
You harmed my being, stole my precious gem, my heart,

Your sight was nothing but darkness,
that which was engulfed in light,
I believed in a single glimmer of light,
but now that glimmer spreads pain,
No matter how I feign,
the bruises are too deep to be washed by rain,
Now all I feel is sadness engulfed in absolute madness
All my heart can do now is to scream so much in pain,

I gave you my heart,
and return you handsomely paid back with hurt,
And my trust, all along I felt it was love, only for it to be dust,
I trusted you when it was dark, only to feel it back with a stab,
Now, you have left me drowning in agony, what did I do wrong,
Was I not sweet enough,
or better was my love so weak to fall in a single cough,

Am all alone in a broken life, shattered greatly to the core,
I feel nothing at all, and love exist no more, broken to the floor,
I can't listen to my anymore, I am not that strong, I died,
A feeling of lost stand, so broken off, it hurts so much,
Let me free, I need you no more, for I am broken like a wall.

©Pamwrites

UNTIL WE MEET AGAIN

How swift time flies, and as dust vanish,
Day in feels like meeting you were my fate
And losing you was not in my control,
I can only say, loving you was, but my decision.

It only hurts that you were my soulmate,
And it hurts even more that you made me No love,
Sorry for being selfish, that I refused to let you go,
It's just that you were that sunshine that fired on me.

I am cold, and my body is so sore
My knees are weak, and my heart so weary,
My heart stops beating, my spirit has died
And I am sorry, I cannot hold the candle anymore.

I cry for my perishing soul, but my weak heart
Refuses to live on without a dream, it wanders to wake,
I am not looking forward to building anything again
But i hope that you see it, that which is lost

I can't express how hard it is, I hope you see it someday
And when that happens, may you be the cure to this sadness,
It may feel messed, but I wish to decay no more,
Until it is well, I beg to rest, someday we shall start again.

©Pamwrites

A GEM, SO RARE TO ONE

The Stars shone brightest and the moon grew brighter,
For a soldier in a princess was on her way to see light,
The winds blew strong and the skies completely grew calm,
Her presence without sight was but a sight of foreseen gift,

She is that princess of her mom who came on strong without a fuss,
And then guess what, a creeping loud cry, she made,
Wow, it was such a peaceful cry to long for never heard before,
And then she stretched her arms so tiny to touch,

Seemingly trying so hard to see from the laps of closed eyelids,
She opened the gates of blessings a treasure of the heart never hurt,
My super princess a gift so rare and a flower so fair,
A doll never to hurt and a love forever to cherish,

On a day like this nothing felt sweet to touch but your hands,
Nothing felt good to look at but your face,
No name felt exciting to call but your name,
And nothing felt nice to wish for but your health,

And again, on this day, all that feels good is seeing you,
Grow much older to make a swift step,
This day only feels good to know that God has blessed a life in you,
It only feels good hearing that laughter so tenderly sweet,

This day, a wish is one but many,
More life, more smiles and laughter's,
More growth and strides,
More cheekiness but, full
fragrance of life.

20th October,
My hero in mama was born,
My heroine starred the day,
Happy birthday, my heroine, My princess.

©Pamwrites

A WRITER'S PEN

My pen should be that with a magic spell,
Not that spell of an underground tale,
But that spell that controls your mind.
My pen should be that which beams a smile
Like Timothy Wangusa or Maya Angelou,
I want to write what I want to write.
At the end of a line, you should yearn for more,
My words should keep the pages turning,
With utmost eagerness, get glued to the flow,
My pen should vomit those of truth,
Not truth that leaves when it leaves,
But the truth of your truth.

I want to write in a way that takes you to wander
In between the lines you get lost in thy words
For I want to write numberless pages
At the mention of my name, comes a thirst,
The absence of my pen should stir mind chaos
My words should lure lightning from the books
My pen should be a source of wisdom
To the world it should inspire
And without chaos it should reign
Without a dance it should entertain
For a lifetime my pen should live
In the dictionary of writers, it should be.

©Pamwrites

AN ODE TO THE SUN

What a name, that which you possess
At dawn you wake me up to start a new day for me
All day long you walk miles and miles to allow me pass the day,
Without a rest you stand still till the setting base where you rest
When you smile, my world becomes hotter than fire
And when gloomy, thunder raids my territory with much heaviness
In the morning, your beauty lights up the sky, dazzling like diamond
And in the evening, when you leave, it fades away into the clouds,
Sun, the beauty in thy name is strong in its hands of appearance.

©Pamwrites

HE THAT OWNS

Seeking He in thy kingdom in heaven is that which,
Places he that is righteous in the midst of everlasting peace,
In soundness and thoughts, the most-high guides the soul,
Resting it in His realm of endless boarders of protection,
Indebtly making you a pillar of an everlasting testimony
To those that desire for an everlasting life in his kingdom,
Under the guide of his teachings through his chosen teachers
Actively putting his teachings in the mind for daily experience,
Leaving out the worldly pleasures that may hinder acceptance of his teachings
In the very easy way of honoring Jesus's life as a savior,
Through alleviation from the darkness of the world,
Yearning to endlessly receive his divine blessing for eternal life.

THE VOICE TO RECKON

In his residing emotions, dreams on to pave a path,
Discovering passions and talents that he yearns to attain,
Seeks to excel and just like a river,
directs thoughts towards his passion,
A longing thought of success lingers in his mind woven with care
Amidst the fears and doubts that tend to cloud his way.

Oh, he thinks of owning a house
He must recall and work as hard as a bee
Sweat all his ideas to the growing dream
For he must triumph through his many trials
Upon lessons and desire clamped on with resilience he attacks all

Practicing what he has learnt, for he knows tough days are ahead,
In his fleeting thoughts lies a dream to a bright future.
Unveiling passions, he adores his unfolding dreams,
Making steps so big amidst pressure and doubts
Embracing truth of self-discovery in a world of friendships.

Beckoned on with challenges, finds hope in friends,
Thoughts of transition plunge deep in mind
Ready to dive and ignite emotions stored beneath
His shared secrets between the mind and heart.
He takes plight into his aspirations yearning to tell a story untold.

©Pamwrites

IN MY SHATTERED BEING

When left behind and falling apart
When no feelings left in my heart
And when I have nothing left to show,
I know there's one true arm that stays on.

And when nothing is left to rejoice
My dreams seem to come to an end,
When I cannot count on my tears anymore,
I know there's a wheel that steers me on.

When life feels like nothing to offer me
And all feel so dizzy
Making me vulnerable to pain,
There's she, who provides freedom to my caged being.

She cheers me on to the end point
A solace of my kind,
Who dares to change the shape and tides of the hurdles.
A voice of my conscious soul, who finds my lost spark.

©Pamwrites

ODE TO BRASSIERE

Oh, my wonderful friend, With tiny little fingers
Yet holding so much with just two porched bags
A store of the mighty "paw paws"
Where did you run to Is it under the bed
Or at the bath tub Did you jump in the closet?
I need you now. I am searching,
I am losing my mind, Oh, my friend,
We need to go; you know I need your company.
Oh, here you are at the cupboard,
Next time don't do that So, we won't be late
Or we might lose him. You know,
The one who holds my heart,
Just right next to where you sit,
Covering it all for might So, they don't jump
And off the blouse they go.

YOUR HONOUR

It is my duty to say thank you,
For you have given me life.
It is my pleasure to give you my worship,
For you are the emblem of life.
The owner of breath. Your honor,
You take me from unknown to known
It is my duty to savor the taste of the moment
To relish in thanksgiving
And to bow in the manner of the season.

Your honor It is my duty,
For all the morning and night
The food that you provide
I say thank you. Your honor,
It with grace that we are embraced
It is with Joy that we smile
With love that we thrive,
And it is my duty
That I give you your honor.

WEIGHT BENEATH

It is drowning me Deep underneath my thoughts,
I cannot move on It has clapped my wings
I lag behind in your memories and sigh on with your image.
I struggle to swim on, But the new waters taste salty
Not sweet like the one We dived in together.
Debris block my way And I have nowhere to turn to.
Way a head looks dark and behind looks even darker,
All clouded, I cannot go on, and I cannot go back
For behind is hollowed and front looks doomed.
This weight is heavy. Set me free allow me fly.
Release me from vagueness Let me see the light ahead
One which calls.

©Pamwrites

STILL HEADING ON

Several times Over the ages,

My heart ponders Neatly and plainly

About my journey, Maybe I should alight,

But have I even boarded? Utterly confused in my thought,

Linens of hope still linger within, Intense questions jots in,

Smoothing my heart with "It shall be Okay"

My journey is still far great, I rest.

WITHERED AFFECTION

I heard them, the words you said,

Don't you think they were sweet nothings?

I hate it, That crooked smile,

It tore me apart, goodbye.

SEASONS GONE

The emblem of our past times keeps up with me,

The times when life seemed so soft to admire,

When we had no worries of tomorrow,

Those days are no more but memories,

Can we go back to the times we lost?

TRAPPED INNOCENCE

Home,
A place where a soul desires to settle
Yet mine in it perished and weakened,
A place where a heart warms up
Yet mine in its troubled and squeezed,
A haven of peace, with whispers of love
Yet mine in it a cage to my breath, engulfed in darkness.

With everyday screams wallowing over my head,
A bruised heart from harsh words sharp like a blade,
This, just because I had no mama to warm up my heart,
Echoes of curses sung upon my head day to night,
All because I had no mama to change my story,
Every day pain piercing through to my chest,

Every day tears washing my face and leaving a line so white and pale,
A child of warmth now a sunken bait to food,
The sound of footsteps on my door sends shivers
Fear creeps in worrying of the unkind hands that strike and peel
A voice raging with words so harsh like a whip
An everyday destruction of innocent thought of a home.

Everyday prayer of a child unheard,
Just a little bit of peace, a little bit just like them with their mama,
The yearning for comfort just likes a dream forgotten,
A war of survival must be fought, tomorrow is bright

All these just silent thoughts suffocating me in my pains
Wishing for a flicker of warmth, love so cherished.
Home,
A place not to give up love and hope,
Resilience to pain a life without it is no gain,
A must to rise, wipe off the gloom and bloom,
It is just for a while, just like seasons it comes and goes,
A child with a heart so shattered must then strike
Break the silent shield and build a path off the mask of a smile

It is never the end, stand up break the chains of darkness, build up the light,
Break the chains of silent tears, cry it out loud,
Rise a voice and make courage your shield,
Rekindle hope like a surviving cactus in the woods of Sahara
Make your scars a story to be told of your past,
Rise your head high, flee captivity of fear.

Forget the wagging that gave you sores
Focus on the lease of a single ray of hope that shines up
It shall surely reach you and illuminate that darkness engulfing you
For a fall jets in a new color of hope and things shall get to start a new
And it shall be a new time of your life just like a spring wonderful day
It will be a time to feel good, bloom and say it is time to cheer.

©Pamewrites

SOLEMN PEN

When weighed down with emotions
And my mind seems so blurry to make sense,
Peace slides in through the lines of words
Flowing smoothly in my mind like a river
That flows through the smooth rock beds,
Free of heavy hindrance boulders
Finding a true solace in the unwinding ideas.

And when darkness overshadows my light,
When I seem not to see the day right,
My mind smoothers through to the ideas
That explore my unwavering feelings
Straying my worries behind in its depth
Zeroing it all to memories so true and unseen
In the joys of the words, lined up in symphony.

My pen itches to patch up my thoughts
Drown my sorrows and make my mind serene
Conveying that which is deeply heavy
Beneath the ore of the unmentioned.
Liberating the sour and unveiling the hidden truths
And reigning all in their full surge
Where I find rest as they all fade and peace meet.

Poetry so pure and tranquil My cure of unwinding burdens
A heavy refuge to my wails A pen of solemn magnitude
Breathing out my deepest burdens

Injecting my inner grace with peace
I, in the solemn pen finds my peace, lies my medication.

In lines of rhythm, I find a melody to my heart
Through to the waves of language, a convening thought reside
Unravelling the hidden sparks and mending the broken peace
Without a heavy do, lines flow to give a blessed soul
A rest where there's no crease,
Journeyed in words I find comfort without a bed.
A solemn pen, the road of tranquil lines.

@Pamwrites

BAD BUD

I see it growing and my heart aches in pain,
Why can't we refrain from this act so plain?
It is a wind that sweeps us off from our roots
Immersing the life lived by our fore ancestors
Into its dark modes, sniffing its morality off.
I shed tears when I see it's shoot becoming leafy
Making branches allover watered in without concern.

Now it's when she puts that cap backwards,
Or when he puts on those high-heeled shoes,
It is okay when she "sags" that trouser to its bottom
And walks on bouncing forward and sideways
with her hands in between her thighs,
Is it okay for him to plait his hair and put those earrings
He is even being praised when he puts on
a dress and makes up his eye lashes.

Why have we allowed the bad bud
to grow its shoots everywhere?
Washing away those that we held so dear,
I can't even put on my all seven-colored clothes anymore,
For I fear might he labelled a "rainbow" community,
I might be discriminated and stoned if I say I love a rainbow,
Forgetting that my fore fathers treasured its appearance,
Now when I look at the sky, I mumble never to be heard.
Treasured memories have been clouded by a smokey wave,
It has even become an offense to hug my fellow girl

For I might wake up to the news that breaks my dignity
This bad bud has labelled my brothers wrong for sharing a room,
The society can no longer smile when they walk together
Fear and doubt have flooded the street of relationships that prevail,
Is it not okay anymore?

Can't we just shun away all that erodes that which is mighty
And embrace all our roots that makes us whole?
Can we not divide ourselves into colors and embrace what we owned?
Let's shape our thinking into the liking of what is true to life,
Let's give respect to brother and sisterhood as it was before the bud grew,
And keep the memory of the space true to its true identity,
For i want to shine without any label when I put on my multicolored dress.

The growing bad bud must be tamed I need space to feel free of my doing,
The bad bud must be peeled off Give respect to God's choice of relationship
Keep life together as it was and let the freedom prevail
So that my "brother" who plaits hair is not given a label.
And my sister who "sags" is not called otherwise.

©Pamwrites

LET THEM KNOW

Let them know I am trying to be there.

Let them know life is not fair, you must toil hard like that ant

Push up to the hill to get your share Let them know I will not ignore my strength,

I will move up high to pave my path Walk on today and come back tomorrow for more,

Stride on behind my steps till I score.
Let them know I won't give up,

Not until I have had it to a pulp,
for I must work extra hard to reach

But by not breaching the codes of the rich.
Let them know I am coming,

My time is running, but I must reach the Centre for I am a hunter.
Let them know.

© Pamwrites

GIVE ME ATTENTION, LISTEN TO ME

When I called out no one cared
Because they considered me an outcast.
I cried to be heard,
But my voice echoed back like a fist.
Why am I different?

Why am I too different to make sense?
I felt lonely by myself
With nights shorter and days longer,
Darkness upon the sunrise,
I thought of peace in the air.

I paced hard in my mind and said,
What a better way to feel the peace
To uproot the unwanted
And what to have people think of me?
Ooh, I got it!

A smile amidst unseen pain flows
Maybe I will get the attention
Once I hear no more.
I will have minds under my feet,
What a better way to have a heart's desire!

I thought of having peace
And I found it away between the dark,
With my mind racing hard on.
Decisively, I rest on my chair,
Never to wake up for I found peace

Away from the pretentious of the living.
I now rest within my walls
Where no one lingers but me,
It makes me happy, I rest on

©Pam@writes

RANJANA RAI

COUNTRY: BHUTAN

WHY DO I WRITE POETRY?

I write poetry to share my heart's whispers, painting feelings with words that linger. It's my soul's expression, a heartfelt confession.

WHAT IS YOUR MESSAGE TO THE WORLD:

Pen kindness, let empathy flow, in written tales, unity and understanding grow. Through words, we weave a tapestry of connection and embrace the power of writing for collective reflection.

CHAPTER SIXTEEN
RANJANA RAI

SELF RESPECT

In shadows deep, where secrets reside,
A soul unfolds, on life's thrilling ride.
With dreams that dance in moonlit streams,
I am the author of my vivid dreams.

Through valleys low and mountains high,
I journey on beneath the boundless sky.
A tapestry is woven with joy and strife,
I am the protagonist of my own life.

In laughter's echo and tears that fall,
I find the rhythm that binds us all.
A symphony played on heartstrings true,
I am the melody that resonates through.

With every step, a tale unfolds,
A story written, of courage that molds.
In the book of time, each page turned,
I am the narrator, and my spirit yearned.

Ranjana Rai
Bhutan BT

FRIENDSHIP'S ETERNAL MELODY

In the garden of companionship, seeds we sow,
Through sunlit days and when shadows grow.
A tapestry woven with laughter and tears,
Friendship's melody lasts through the years.

Hand in hand, we navigate life's maze,
Together we weather both nights and days.
A symphony of trust, a bond so deep,
In friendship's embrace, our spirits keep.

Through seasons changing, and storms that pass,
True friends endure, like a looking glass.
Reflections of kindness, loyalty, and grace,
In this sacred bond, hearts find their place.

So, let's cherish the moments, come what may,
For in the arms of friendship, we find our way.
Through joy and sorrow, till the journey's end,
Forever united, side by side, my friend.

Ranjana Rai

LOVE

In twilight's tender, soft embrace,
Love whispers secrets, face to face.
A dance of hearts, entwined, divine,
A symphony of souls, forever entwined.

Through stormy seas and the calmest nights,
Love weathers all, ignite the lights.
In laughter's joy and sorrow's tears,
Love's melody transcends the years.

With gentle touch and words so kind,
Love blooms in hearts, a tie that binds.
Through valleys low and mountains high,
Love's journey soars, a boundless sky.

In every beat, a shared refrain,
Love's rhythm echoes, free from pain.
A timeless tale, forever told,
Love's flame is eternal, never cold.

Ranjana Rai

EDUCATION'S GUIDING STARS

In halls of learning, minds ignite,
A journey vast, a boundless flight.
Books unfold their wisdom's tale,
In education's timeless trail.

Teachers weave a guiding thread,
Through realms of thought where dreams are bred.
Curiosity, a flame untamed,
In every eager mind proclaimed.

The classroom hums with knowledge's song,
A symphony where minds grow strong.
From lessons learned, a future's sown,
In education's garden, brightly grown.

So let us cherish the gift of insight,
For in learning's dance, hearts take flight.
Education's beacon, a guiding star,
Illuminating paths near and far.

Ranjana Rai

PARENTAL LOVE

In the quiet dawn of parenthood's embrace,
Whispers of love in each tender trace.
A lullaby of sacrifice they sing,
In the cradle of life, their echoes ring.

Through sleepless nights and endless days,
Parents sculpt dreams in myriad ways.
Guiding steps with unwavering care,
Their love is a fortress beyond compare.

In laughter's dance and tearful rain,
A timeless bond that will be sustained.
Roots entwined, a familial tree,
Branches reaching, a legacy free.

So, cherish the garden of love they sow,
In every sunrise, in sunset's glow.
For parents, the architects of our start,
Forever reside in the soul's beating heart.

Ranjana Rai

PASSION

In the heart's deep embrace, passion ignites,
A flame that dances through endless nights.
Bold dreams take flight on wings of fire,
As fervor's whispers stoke desire.

Through the canvas of life, colors blend,
Passion's melody is a song without an end.
In the dance of souls, an intimate art,
A symphony composed from the heart.

With each heartbeat, a passionate plea,
A rhythm that echoes, wild and free.
In the tapestry of time, passion weaves,
A legacy of love that eternally believes.

So let passion guide, a compass true,
A force that paints the world anew.
In the garden of life, let passion bloom,
A fragrant flower, dispelling gloom.

Ranjana Rai

WRITING HEALS

In the quiet realm of paper and ink,
A solace found, where troubles shrink.
Words weave magic, a soothing balm,
In the dance of lines, healing's calm.

Through the valleys of heartache and pain,
Writing whispers, breaking every chain.
Emotions penned, a cathartic release,
Healing blooms like a gentle peace.

The poet's hand, a miraculous grace,
Transforms wounds into a sacred space.
In the cadence of verses, a melody sings,
A healing symphony that mends all things.

So, let the pen dance, let the words flow,
In the alchemy of writing, sorrows bow.
For on the parchment of dreams and despair,
Healing is etched, a remedy rare.

Ranjana Rai

SMILE

In the dawn's gentle embrace, a smile unfurls,
A sunlit dance of joy in a world of pearls.
Contours of happiness cheeks a rosy hue,
Whispers of serenity, like morning dew.

Midday's warmth, a radiant smile's embrace,
Chasing shadows, leaving no trace.
Laughter blooms in fields of golden gleam,
A symphony of joy, a sunbeam dream.

Twilight whispers secrets, a smile's twilight,
Painting the sky in hues of soft light.
Eyes twinkle like stars, a cosmic grace,
A smile's journey through time and space.

As night descends, a crescent moon's smile,
Guardian of dreams in the quiet aisle.
Silent echoes of joy in the moonlit mile,
A serene lullaby, a timeless smile.

Ranjana Rai

BHUTANESE GIRL

In the land of dragons, where mountains touch the sky,
I am a Bhutanese girl, with dreams that soar high.
Amidst prayer flags dancing in the Himalayan breeze,
I find strength in my roots, grounded by ancient trees.

With grace in my steps, adorned in vibrant Kira's embrace,
I carry tales of culture, a heritage to trace.
In the whispers of dzongs and the rivers that swirl,
I proudly declare, "Yes, I am a Bhutanese girl."

Through rice terraces green, and monasteries old,
I weave stories of tradition, in threads of gold.
In the rhythm of folk songs, my heart finds its twirl,
A melody proclaiming, "Yes, I am a Bhutanese girl."

With eyes that reflect the stars' ethereal gleam,
I'm a symphony of joy in this Himalayan dream.
In the kingdom of happiness, where banners unfurl,
I stand tall, singing, "Yes, I am a Bhutanese girl."

Ranjana Rai

BHUTAN'S BEAUTY UNVEILED

In the heart of the Himalayas, Bhutan's grace,
Mountains cradle tales, a sacred embrace.
Dzongs stand tall, whispering ancient lore,
A kingdom's beauty, like never before.

Valleys adorned with prayer flags that dance,
Whispers of tranquility, a mystical trance.
Gross National Happiness, a guiding light,
Bhutan's beauty, a symphony so bright.

Monasteries cling to cliffs, touch the sky,
Where spirituality soars, eagles fly.
Nature's canvas, vibrant and pure,
Bhutan's allure, forever endure.

Dragon Kingdom, where traditions thrive,
Gentle souls, keeping nature alive.
Amidst the peaks, a serene decree,
Bhutan's beauty is timeless and free.

Ranjana Rai

PEACE

In twilight's hush, the world takes a sigh,
Where tranquil whispers softly comply.
Beneath the moon's gentle, silver fleece,
Dances the symphony, the melody of peace.

Mountains stand as guardians, silent and grand,
Their peaks touch the heavens, a tranquil land.
Rivers weave tales, a serenity release,
Nature's lullaby, the essence of peace.

Amidst the chaos, a haven untold,
Where compassion blooms, a love manifold.
Harmony's embrace, conflicts cease,
Unity's tapestry, the quilt of peace.

In hearts united, a flame ever bright,
Igniting hope, dispelling the night.
Together we find, that as struggles decrease,
The timeless refuge, the sanctuary of peace.

Ranjan Rai

LIFE'S LESSONS UNFOLD

In life's vast book, lessons unfold,
Each chapter rich with tales untold.
Through trials faced and challenges met,
Wisdom blooms, a cherished asset.

Adversity, a stern but just guide,
Teaches strength, where shadows hide.
With every stumble, a chance to rise,
Lessons learned beneath the skies.

In the tapestry of time we weave,
Each lesson, a thread, helps us believe.
From triumphs sweet to failures' sting,
In lessons, we find the songs that sing.

So let the pages turn, the journey sway,
For in each lesson, we find our way.
A symphony of growth, a dance of grace,
In learning's embrace, we find our place.

Ranjana Rai

ASPIRATION

In dreams we weave, aspirations bold,
A tapestry of tales yet to be told.
Through skies of hope, our spirits soar,
To realms unknown, forevermore.

The heart's desire, a flame untamed,
Igniting paths where destinies are named.
Aspirations rise on wings of might,
Guiding us through the darkest night.

In fields of vision, ambitions bloom,
A garden where possibilities loom.
With each step forward, we transcend,
Our aspirations are a journey without end.

On the canvas of life, dreams unfurl,
Aspirations dance a waltz with the world.
In the symphony of time, let us compose,
A melody of dreams that forever grows.

Ranjana Rai

HUMANITY'S TAPESTRY

In a world of myriad hues, we stand,
Humanity's tapestry is woven by hand.
Diverse threads in a cosmic design,
A dance of souls, unique and fine.

Through trials and triumphs, we unite,
In the symphony of day and night.
Kindred spirits on this earthly ride,
Bound by dreams, in life's stride.

Yet shadows linger, whispers of despair,
In our shared journey, love repairs.
Empathy's embrace, a healing balm,
Humanity's heartbeat, a soothing psalm.

Let compassion guide our collective quest,
For in each heart, a universe rests.
Through storms and sunshine, hand in hand,
Together we thrive, a tapestry grand.

Ranjana Rai

GRATITUDE

In the quiet moments, gratitude blooms,
A whispered thanks, like fragrant perfumes.
For kindness shared, a heartfelt embrace,
In gratitude's dance, we find solace and grace.

Through seasons of life, a chorus of thanks,
Echoing gratitude in rivers and banks.
For friendships true and love that abounds,
In the language of gratitude, joy resounds.

With each sunrise, a new day to savor,
A symphony of thanks, a heartfelt flavor.
For lessons learned and challenges faced,
Gratitude's warmth, an embrace embraced.

So, thank you, a melody that lingers on,
In the tapestry of life, like dawns first drawn.
For moments cherished, both big and small,
In gratitude's embrace, we stand tall.

Ranjana Rai

RAINBOW

Upon the canvas of the sky, a vibrant arc displayed,
A symphony of hues unveiled, in colors bright arrayed.
From red to violet, a journey unfolds,
The rainbow's dance of light, a story to be told.

Bathed in sunlight's tender kiss, droplets play their part,
Transforming rain to artistry, a masterpiece of heart.
Each color whispers tales untold, a promise in the air,
A bridge connecting dreams and earth, a sight beyond compares.

In azure heavens, arcs embrace, a celestial embrace,
A promise painted on the clouds, a glimpse of nature's grace.
Through storm and shower, hope persists, a beacon in the rain,
The rainbow's radiant promise, a reminder of joy regained.

So, let your spirit soar and sing, like colors on display,
For in the arc of the rainbow, hope is never far away.
A tapestry of wonder, a gift from sky to sod,
The rainbow's radiant beauty, a testament to God.

Ranjana Rai

NATURE

In fields of green, where sunlight weaves,
Nature's tapestry, a dance of leaves.
Whispers of wind through towering trees,
A symphony of life, carried on gentle breeze.

Mountains stand as ancient sentinels bold,
Their peaks adorned in moonlight's gold.
Rivers weave tales, a liquid song,
Nature's melody, pure and strong.

Meadows adorned in wildflower hue,
Butterflies waltz, a ballet in view.
Underneath the canvas of the sky,
Nature's masterpiece, where wonders lie.

Oceans vast, an endless embrace,
Waves whisper secrets, leaving no trace.
Nature's rhythm, a timeless rhyme,
A sacred dance, throughout all time.

Ranjana Rai

MUSIC

In melodies that dance on air,
Music weaves its magic rare.
Notes entwined, a symphony's embrace,
A timeless journey, boundless grace.

Rhythmic heartbeat, a steady drum,
Strings that hum, emotions strum.
Harmony whispers in the night,
A sonorous symphony taking flight.

Lyrics tell stories, a soulful song,
Echoes of joy, where sorrows belong.
Piano keys paint a canvas vast,
Music's power, forever steadfast.

From classical whispers to modern beat,
Music's language, universally sweet.
In its embrace, emotions unfold,
A symphony of life, untold.

Ranjana Rai

FLOWER

In gardens bright with colors fair,
A bloom emerges, light as air.
Petals dance in the gentle breeze,
Whispering secrets to the trees.

Sun-kissed hues, a vibrant array,
Each petal tells a tale of the day.
Blossoms open, a delicate plea,
Nature's art in sweet harmony.

Morning dew adorns the bloom,
Glistening in the soft day's room.
With grace, the flower stands tall,
A living poem, nature's call.

As twilight falls and shadows play,
The flower dreams until the day,
Awaiting dawn's soft, tender kiss,
In nature's symphony of bliss.

Ranjana Rai

BETRAYAL

In shadows cast by trust's own fleeting light,
A dance with shadows, veiled in the night.
Whispers echo, deceit takes its hold,
Betrayal's tale, a story yet untold.

Once allies, hearts entwined, now apart,
A fracture deepens, tearing at the heart.
Promises shattered, like glass on the floor,
Betrayal's sting, a wound to the core.

The Judas kiss, a symbol of deceit,
A bond severed, bitter and replete.
Eyes that once held loyalty's gaze,
Now mirrors of betrayal's haunting maze.

Yet, from the wreckage, strength may rise,
A phoenix born where trust demise.
In the ashes, resilience takes its stand,
For even in betrayal, hope commands.

Ranjana Rai

LAVIN OWENDE (THE NEEVE)

COUNTRY: KENYA

La-ki is a writer and poet from Kenya a country in East Africa. She began writing at a tender age and has been writing for 15 years having found an outlet and a way of therapy in poetry.

CHAPTER SEVENTEEN
LAVIN OWENDE (THE NEEVE)

INTRODUCTION

Immortal poetry, immortal me
Lucky La-ki

I'm the tree that grows in the suburbs
I'm the green that beautifies the desert
I'm the oasis
That quenches the thirst of the desert soil
I'm the lucky La-ki

I'm the pen that inks everlasting poetry
I'm the pen that immortalized every moment
Am an African Mogul
Whose name shall live
In pages of literature generations
That shall come after me
I'm the lucky La-ki

I'm the pen
Born of pure talent
Drunk in words, high in flowing lines
I'm the eternal pen

And my foot prints

Permanent on the sands of literature

I'm the lucky La-ki

I'm the first version of me

Baba's favorite descendant

And as his blood flows in my veins

So, does greatness

In form of rhythm and rhyme

An immortal being

That shall live forever

In the pagesG of her work

I'm the lucky La-ki

© La-ki

Immortal poetry, immortal me

CARRYING THE WEIGHT

Ugly pictures at the back of my mind
Tear drops overflow I smile from the outside
But no one really knows the burden that rests upon me
In the deepest corner of my heart, I carry the weight

My entire being shivers at the thoughts
Episodes of unforgotten nightmares
I'd cry myself to sleep
Thinking of the in imaginable
My oh my I carry the weight

I whisper it in the pages of my books
Thinking it could help ease my pain
Hoping it will help release the anxiety
And I'll somehow tackle my greatest fears

I carry the weight
Painful incidents I can never forget
Painful puzzles I can never solve
And the anger that builds in me
Each time I face episodes of this unknown fear
And I crave talking to someone
Who would understand me
But no, I fear judgement Critics and rejection
So, every minute I find myself Alone
I try to resist
But still, I carry the weight

I carry the weight
Of nursing scars in my soul
And sometimes I get antidotes
That end up worsening my wounds
And each time I cry
I think of the possibilities
Of never finding solutions
I think of the possibilities
Of when a time will come
And I'll feel overburdened
And when I try to lift the weights
My wrinkled arms will give in
And I'll drop it to the floor
I'll take a deep breath
My last poem inked with pure emotion
Letter of a goner
One who wore a mask of a smiley face
But deep down
Was drained by the weights she carried
But was strong enough
To keep the faith

A La-ki original

ME TO ME

Those traumas
They still keep me up at night
Those traumas
They keep me inking my hours away
Words I wish I knew then
Maybe they would keep you going

Hands were tied
Blamed when you were the victim
Those mornings
You woke up with swollen eyes

Those traumas
That trigger tears out of you
Those things that leave you trembling
Those fears that leave you lost in thoughts
Those things that toughened you
And the walls you built
To protect your fragile self

Don't know how to rectify the past
Don't know how to reverse the clock
Maybe I'd choose a different path
Those traumas, you didn't deserve
You were just a flower

That flourished in a thorny field
As I walk in your shoes each day
I'll find ways to heal the inner you

© La-ki
Walking in her shoes.

OUR FOREVER IS FORBIDDEN

Once again
Tell me those beautiful lies

Our forever is forbidden
We both know it's harmless Meet me at the cave
And the walls that surround
The secrets of our beautiful sin

Melted by the words you say
Melting at your touch
My heart for take away
Served it hot
A pinch of salt
Save some for the next one
Hold on to our intimate moments

You ask why I'm hopeless
I once spelt eternity
But tomorrow never came
I'm hopeful
One foot inside
Left with everlasting poetry
I once spelt divinity
That one healed me
Don't remember her name
Forbidden love is sweet
Moments of tender kisses

I'll immortalize certain moments
Live in these pages like it's all I have
Poetic justice will be my end game

© La-ki
A million Pages of everlasting poetry

REMEMBER ME

They say
Moments become memories
Poets immortalize the special ones
I'll keep you safe
Tell your story
In these pages
Whisper softly
The secrets that charmed me

I'll recall your smile
Immortalize your existence
Those beautiful moments
That melt me
Though I know you don't care much
Still hope you remember me

Remember my laughter
My endless unfunny jokes
You never laugh at any
Remember my pissed face
And how my cheeks swell
How my lips frown
Remember me
If I made your heart beat for a second
Remember my smile
Remember me
Those beautiful passing winds

Saw the end at the beginning
When listening to those songs
You play on repeat
The ones you liked to play
Ice in your chest
Unable to melt it
Say you'll remember me

I'll REMEMBER YOU

Can't believe you are gone
I wish we had more time
I can't believe you are gone
I wish to see you again
Listen to you tell us
The stories from your days

I'll remember you
Will remember your smile
And the long trips
That brought us to you
I'll remember the nights
Sitting by your side
Laughing and talking
About the things that bonded us

I'll remember you
The lessons you taught me
To work hard in class
Be the best for you
And there was always a reward
To the best of performances
Told me I was bright
And bright people have bright futures

I'll remember you
And how safe it was by your side

Sheltered under your wing
You have gone too soon
Who will check on me
Ask me to get the best grades???
My heart is heavy
Still every day I love
I'll remember you

© La-ki
Memories of the departed souls

SOMEWHERE IN THE SKY

A cloud floating by
Buried a piece of me
Under the red lump that covered you

Roses so pretty
Still remember your smile
Those songs that keep our memories
Help me finish the lyrics
Chanting to old stories
Somewhere in the skies
A star that shines on me

I have all your memories
The jokes from our childhood days
The paths we founded
While finding ourselves
Lost at crossroads
Don't know how to leave your side
By your grave side I hum a lullaby
Hoping you'll wake up
Pinch me say it was a dream

Somewhere in the sky

I'm searching for your smile

The good ones join the angels

I bet you were the best of all

I loved you

God loved you more

He plucked the prettiest flower

Thorns left pricking my heart

Rest in peace

© La-ki
Memories of the departed souls

SOMEDAY I'll FORGIVE YOU

I always picture the day
I'll take the leap of faith
Still, I live
One step forward
Two steps behind

I lose the best of all
My blood didn't drain the poison
I relieve the trauma
Each time my heart beats for another

I dream of the day
It wouldn't matter
When my best moments
Wouldn't warrant me to give you a call
And tell you about it all

My hearts chronicle
My pens ink
Wouldn't spell your name
I lie to myself
One, too many times

Someday it will be gone with the wind
I know I'll forgive you
And I'll forgive me too
Still finding pieces of me
All wrecked but going strong

© La-ki
The Tales of a Poet's Deepest Secrets

RUNNING TO THE CROSS

Running from myself
The world is after me
Praying for your grace
Shine your light on me

Haunted by the dark days
Losing a grip of life
Calling out your name
Lift me from this dark hole

The world against me
Painting me black
Their backs turned to me
I cry to you
A sigh from a hopeless soul
A cry for help
It's me against them
I walk unshielded

I try to mumble a prayer
The wind makes me shiver
Losing a grip of life
Losing pieces of me
Losing my mind
Losing my whole life
I call out your name
Between breaths of uncertainty
Save me from myself
Let your will be done

© La-ki
A sinner's plea

INCARNATION OF THE PROMISE

God gave us a lifetime
Incarnation of a promise
In sickness and in health
The vows we mumbled that day
My heart to hold
You kept the promise

Every day by my side
Asked for a family
You gave me an entire generation
And my babies got your eyes
The grand babies

A continuation of the
dream we shared
God gave us a lifetime
He chose the best for me
Caring and understanding
You gave me your all
Your youth and beyond

Still loved me like your
life depended on it

God gave us a lifetime

You were an answered prayer

A shoulder to lean on

I never lacked by your side

He gave us a lifetime

Blessings beyond what we asked for

Dear future poetic predictions

Pieces of us.

I PROMISE YOU

I promise you
I'll give this a lifetime
Every day by your side
Finding pieces of us

I promise you
I'll help you chase your dreams
I'll cheer you on
Every venture you partake

I promise you
I'll give you a lifetime
A family of our own
A generation to carry our name

I promise you
I'll be by your side
In every season
Till my last breath

I promise you
I'll give you my all
Share your visions

And toil hard each day
To build a strong foundation
For our future generations

I promise you
We'll remember this day
We'll remember these promises
And we'll thank the Almighty and whisper
It's the incarnation of the promise

© La-ki
Pieces of us

DEAR FUTURE

They say tomorrow's a mystery
So, I spend today
Walking on eggshells
Lest I face a future of pure regrets
And an anthem called
I wish I knew

Dear future
Whisper silently in my ear
The secrets you hold for me
I promise I'd never betray you
In another mouth you'd never hear

I feel scared
Each and every day
Wondering how, when and where
I'd find myself lost in a gaze
Trying to figure out my tomorrow
Yet my today stays unraveled

Dear future
Judge me not
For the life l lead today
Erase the mistakes
I make down this path I walk
I'm a victim of circumstance
My life isn't what I ever pictured it to be

Dear future forgets the path I walk
Go easy on me
I'm a mess as it is
Can't take more blows
From this thing called life
Warm my heart with promises
Of a good life and prominence
Swear that's what am aiming at
Swear that's what I'm working towards

Dear future
Let my path be full of strangers
Sent by fate
To be my destiny helpers
Lead me into the right paths
Paths that bring me closer
To a safer space
To achieve all that
I'm sweating my youth away for

Dear future
Show me a picture of yourself
Dim or even blurred
I'd appreciate
For I'll know what way to take
Which friends to keep
And those that dim the light
Of a brighter you
I'll bid them goodbye

Make sure they stop dragging me behind

Dear future
I only wish
To get a glimpse of you
But as I daydream
Painting pictures of you
I hope some of my dreams
Will definitely comes true
Dear future I'm fragile
So, I'll leave you In the hands
Of my creator

©La-ki

DEAR ME I LOVE YOU TO COLOURS

Feeling the raindrops
Dampen the garment on my skin
The soil stains my cloth
I rock a fragile smile
Tears at the corner of my eye

I watch the clouds cover the sun
The sounds of the winds blowing
Penetrating my hair strands
Making me shiver with cold

It's a passing storm
No showers, no rains
But the colors fill the sky
And I carry my flag with pride.

As the rainbow in the sky
Signifies the end of the storms
The flag in my hand
Signifies the end of it all
Of the shame, of the fear
Of the inability to stand tall
To carry my flag with pride

The flag of my identity
Which I raise today

And as the wind blows into it
I bow down with respect
I salute my flag
I discover my purpose
I'm proud to be me
I carry my flag with pride

I watch it wave
A symbol of freedom
Like the rainbow in the sky
Untouchable and unchangeable
Mark the colors of the rainbow
Mark the colors of my flag
That's the color
Of the blood in my veins

Out and proud
I carry my flag with pride

©La-ki

COLOURING THIS LIFE 1

Parallel world's
You found healing
In the Bossom of my heart
I play your favorite song on repeat
Living in the moment
In your arms
I find comfort

I swear to you
We won't fall in love
We'll live to enjoy
Drowning in the thrill
Of these moments

Mixing colors
Coloring this life
Perfect combination
Painting with no expectations
Of what a perfect picture should be
Our only motive
Living to explore
The us that exists

My heart beat so fragile
Like a pin hits the floor
Disappearing in the colors
Calling out your name

Begging you to tighten your grip on me
Feel myself shiver
Feel the colors stick on my skin
We'll wash it all away someday
We'll find ourselves someday

My fragile hand in yours
Getting a grip of it
Getting a grip of me
Regard La-ki regard
That's the smell of paint
Paint-stained garments

One last kiss for the road
Heading to an unknown destination
Butterflies in my stomach
Thinking of the unknown
It's like living a daydream
Breaking rules
Falling but not falling
Finding ourselves
Hearts beating the same tune
Shivers

Painting the skies
Colors of a flag we carry
Not seeking anyone's approval
Not seeking recognition
Live in the moment you'd say

Making me take in every moment
Making me feel
Life's just about us
Living this forbidden life
In the midst of it all
Gallons of paint
Show me the color of passion
Gallons of paint
Write on me
In my heart like a tattoo
Walking into tomorrow barefoot
Hoping we won't wake up
Drunk in the love
That we both don't want
But like you'd put it
It's all Vibes and Inshallah

© La-ki
© Sashy (coloring this life)

COLOURING THIS LIFE 2

Colors between these pages
Paintings of ended misery
Moping the last tear drop
The sky is blue
And my heart melted
I woke up in the arms of another
And I saw a smile light up my face

A whisper into my ear
I cover my face blushing
I giggle at an inside joke
Cheek bones full of color
Live in the moment
Coloring this life

Colors in rhythm and rhyme
Colors of poetic Justice
Unprescribed medicine
Try not to fall in love
Deep breath
Take it slow
So, we can last long

Whisper to me your little secret
Whisper to me
All the good
All the nasty
What are we???

The chosen generation perhaps

Coloring the sky in unknown colors
Coloring these pages of our lives
With beautiful colors
Of unforgettable memories

Holding onto the embrace
Hoping to last a moment longer
Drowning in your natural cologne
Starring into those eyes
That drive desire into me

A little spark of emotion
I find solace in you
A little consolation
A little bit more color

Days of our youth
Secrets we'll keep sealed
In the deepest corners of our hearts
And these picture-perfect memories
A little more color
To the paintings
We'll keep
In the gallery
Of Our life stories

COLORING THIS LIFE 3

At a glance
Tomorrow happening today
A thousand boxes of crayons
Tighten your grip
On my fragile hands
Teach me to color these pages
You and I Coloring this life

The color of your eyes so pretty
Dim the lights
I love the color of the sky
Starless nights
We can see eye to eye

And the words we say
Mouths closed
Eye to eye
Perfect communication
What is the color of passion???

What is the color of passion??
Luminous I'd say
As bright as the flames
Of our unending lustful passion
Passion and power
Lustful and in control
That you own me when you need it
Oh, baby so do I
Color of our youthful days

Secrets we'll take to the grave

Coloring this life
Your name tattooed inside
A part of me
In the colors
Of these flags I carry

Standing tall singing my anthem
A symphony of joy
I see color in your eyes
And I love
The color of the glow
Of your skin

What is the color of love??
Shut me up with kisses
I don't want to talk about the hailstorms
Hold you dear for a minute
Then spend forever cursing you

I don't want to live in the fear
"What ifs" of a tragic ending
So, I live in the moment
Choosing not to define
Is this love or lust It's just us
Coloring this life

Sashy (Coloring this life)

ONLY YOU

End game
I found solace
In the eyes of my forever

Breaking dawn
Of a love story
Certain tales become magic
And ours is the one

Nights without stargazing
The universe agrees
That for us
The stars shall align

Only you
That taught my heart
The rhythm it should beat
An old symphony
From an old poem
Written in the skies

Only you
Who knows me in and out
Still chose me
To walk with
The path to forever

Only you
Who knows my scars
And the burdens of my heart
My soul mates
My best friend

Only you
Who gives me purpose
To be the best version of myself
So, I can deserve
The love that you give me

Only you
That makes it worth
To sweat my youth away
So, we can build a future
Of achieved dreams and endless possibilities

Only you
That gives me the hope
That all my tears shall dry
Ever since I met you
No vacancy
No room for another

Only you
That makes me run to the altar
That I may whisper a prayer
And with every dawn break

I say to the Almighty
Bless me once again father
Like you did the day
You gifted her to me
And I to her
And for every obstacle
Give us the strength to overcome
Come out stronger in person
And stronger in love

A million pages of everlasting poetry

SOMEDAY

Someday
We'll make a toast
To the good old days

We'll laugh at the good
And cheers to the memories we love
And in every page of my book
Congratulatory pieces

Someday
We'll recall
The ghost of our dark days
And every hard time
Will be a testimony
Of all we over came

Someday we'll remember
The paths we walk today
However dark they are
We still have each other
Echoes of laughter
Accolades and more accolades
For we lived through it all
And we became family

©La-Ki

MORNING AWAITS

Nights are long
Nights are lonely
Nights are long
Nights are drowning

Counting down hours
Hoping tomorrow comes
Wishing for sunrise
An oasis to quench
the desert thirsts

Morning waits for you
Holding a future in its hands
No fury, you'll never be sad
Morning waits for the sun
A light in the midst
Of your darkest hours

Morning awaits
To bring you smiles
Walking into sunrise alone
No one by your side

Walking into sunrise
with a smile
Recite a promise
From last night
A poem from your soul

© La-ki
The tales of a poet's deepest secrets

BREAKING DAWN

Wake me up
When it's all over
Wounds of my tales
The pain of my journey
The future starts now
I'll watch my wound become scars
I'll call my scars
My beauty marks

At sunrise
When birds hum
To a song I loved to sing
On my youthful days
Today I walk those steps
Towards a life
I've always dreamt of

Wake me up
And listen to my story
Watch me write a chapter
Of fulfillment, of growth

Watch me at sunrise
Smile on my face,
Scars on my chest
Happiness registered
All over me
A breath of fresh air
Grand awakening
The future starts now

© La-ki

LOVE LIES

I can hear them laugh at me
Their smiles
Stick in my mind
And I ask myself once again
Questions that I'd never want answers to

Coz, you led me to the altar
Put a ring on my finger
In the eyes of the almighty
Asked for mama's blessing
And she put her hand on your head
Giving you a go ahead
To make her daughter yours

Now there are so many buts
I once asked myself
What's the worst that could possibly happen
All my dirty linen
On their cloth lines
And I am not being poetic here
I'm just stating facts

So, they out here
Their guns aiming at us
And you say they only want to break us
But their words are true
Evidence lies in
Scenes we have
Played and replayed in our lives
And I try to convince myself
That you chose me and not them

So, I stand at our bedroom window
Watching you lie on our matrimonial bed
Innocence registered on your face
But guilt written on your soul
And I know you can also hear
Voices of your concubines yelling at me

Asking me to let them in
Coz, you belong to them
Just as much
But I love you selfishly
So once again I send them away.
You smile
Saying I did right
But I know you'll go looking for them
And we'll argue about it again tomorrow
Then I'll face the wall and cry
Before covering my body in garments
So, I can walk on the streets again

Then I'll listen to them
Tell tales
Of the adventures they had with you
Before I come home to you
I'll listen to your lies once again
Before you
Make me yours
And the cycle continues
Scars forming, scars healing.
The journey to our forever....

NOT YOUR COFFIN

The path has never been darker
Hopeless and scared
You think of eternal rest
You wish for eternal peace

Try to mumble a prayer
Words blown by the wind
How does your story end
Walking barefoot on broken glass
Every part of you is lost
Every dream seems like wishful thinking

So, you find yourself cornered
Forty-five to the temple
Best finger on the trigger
But before you let go
It's not your turn
It's not your coffin

The battle against your inner self
The times you curse your existence
It's not yet time to go
The soil is yet to call your name
Don't wave at the coffin seller
That is not your coffin
You look into the mirror
Unable to recognize yourself

But before it all dawns on you
It shall be
Another failed attempt
You will live to see another day
Your time is not yet up
That is not your coffin

© La-ki
The tales of a poet's deepest secrets

DARK DESIRE

One for the road
Take a trip to high water
Heaven is a breath away
Carrying the weight on my shoulders
Heaven is a mile away
Walk with me
Hear my endless tale
Chuckles of laughter
I've walked darker paths
I’ve lost my will to live
A dose of the antidote
Mama calls out for me at sunrise

I yearn to lay there
Body cold, soul gone
Every part of me extinct
Set my legacy ablaze
Heart cold as winter
Moonless midnight
With winds blowing by
Between my pages I whisper
The tales of a poets deepest secrets

Tales of A Poet's Deepest Secrets.

I DON'T NEED CONSOLATION

Grief written all over me
I don't need consolation
Every part of me is torn

I wish I had a river
Would swim to the other side
Death was just a breath away
Didn't get to say goodbye

So many if only
We don't picture epilogue
Death was just a breath away
Didn't get to make you proud

My heart is heavy
Paralyzed with fear
I lack a sense of direction
Wish to hear you one last time
At sunset a star ascends
Cloudy skies

The universe cries with us
My heart is heavy
Osiepa onindo
Wake up baba
Let me hear your voice
One last time

© La-ki
Memories of the departed souls

LET ME LOVE YOU

Let me grow old with you
Bless my mornings with
The gift of your presence

Let me love you
Let me be the one
In your life
Every single day
Together
Let's explore forever

Let me love you
Let me be your woman
The mother of your children
Your lover, your wife

Let me love you
Let me belong to you
Every morning and
Every night,
Let me feel your presence
In my life

Let me love you
Let's stand together
As we chase
All our goals and dreams

Making baby steps
Towards all we
Ever wish to achieve
Let me love you
Let me own you
And I'll give myself to you

Poetry is eternal

SPEAK TO ME

Lover of mine
In eternal whispers
To last a lifetime
Speak to me
In a language

Only we understand
Between unsaid words
Let me read the signs
In your eyes

Speak to me
Your hand on my skin
Between every breath
I get the meaning
I get the reasons
Speak to me

Oh, lover of mine
I'll digest every word
I'll digest every touch
Lock our eyes
Last this life time
And eternity's beyond

A million pages of everlasting poetry
Legacy of The Neeve

EVERLASTING POETRY 1

Birds hum a symphony
A sigh for the fallen pen
No more ink shall flow
The soul has left
But you live
In the pages
You breathed in between
Every day of your life

When a poet dies
Eulogized by other poets
An eagle has flown
Sky was the limit
Now all that's left
Is a legacy
Of everlasting poetry

When a poet dies
We find life
We know their story
Between their tales
The journey of their scars
And the little things
That gave them joy

When a poet dies
They depart from the earth
Only to leave behind

An immortal legacy
Permanent footprints
On the sands of time

© La-ki
A million pages of everlasting poetry

EVERLASTING POETRY 2

I believe I'm immortal
Coz I'll live forever
In the pages of my book
Word for word
Every line flowing
And each stanza
Leading to a forever unknown
Legacy of a girl that once lived

Poetry is eternal
Like the ground I walk on
Lived before I came
Will still live after I depart
For this is food to my soul
Without it I shall slowly leave

One day when I can't lift my pen
And lines can't flow
Bring life into the pages of my books
My eyelids shall stay shut
I shall slowly depart
And my poetry shall live on and on

And if I reincarnate
I shall come back as a poet
Continue where I left
Tell tales with of flowing lines
Highlight the paradox of life
Perhaps I'll be different
And I'll tell different tales
But still, I'll find me
Coz my pen will still bleed similar words

And my art shall be linked
Back to me
Similarities highlighted

Everlasting poetry
For this poetry is my language
And fans shall be my second family
And the lines that flow in my pages
Shall flow into their hearts
And it shall unite us

And when I'm gone
They'll keep telling tales
Of a poet that inked
To keep her sanity intact
Of a poet that breathed
In the stanzas of her work

And a different generation
Shall know of me
Like I tell tales of Edgar Allan
Someone will tell tales of me
And even though
I won't be there to hear them
They'll reach eternity
Till the return
Of the son of man
Coz this poetry is my lover
I call it PIE because
POETRY IS ETERNAL

A La-ki original

POETRY-HOLIC

Am addicted to you, oh poetry
I'm addicted to you
Your ability to capture me, your ability to captivate me
I get lost in the pages of my book
Drunk in words, high in flowing lines
The metaphors the similes the symbolism
I'm a poetry holic, it's the air I breath
My sanity holder, my immortal side
I'm a poetry -holic, without it then i would be lost
My secret keeper, my confidential friend
My antidote, my drug
Am a poetry holic
For this poetry is my language
And the world is my family

A La-ki original

I AM YOU

I am the ink
That flows out of your pen
I am the words
That flow out of your brain
I am the rhythm
That lives in your heart

I am the best part of you
I am poetry, I am you
The light that awakes you at dawn
I am the drive that pushes you
To ink every dawn

I am you
The thirst to drink every drop of it
The thirst to spill it all
The thirst to keep going
Even when the lights flicker
On your eyes
I am you

The pen that inks everlasting poetry
The pen that spelt eternity
In this life
And any that will come
I'll still remain a poet and the last piece
Inked on my death bed

© La-ki
Immortal poetry, immortal me.

DRUNK FROM THE CUP OF PAINS

Oh yes, it is too late
And a crowd shall hum
To a tune I loved
Whispering
In each other's ears
The memories of my smile

Lying peaceful in a hearse
Eulogized by the poetry I wrote
Soon to be forgotten
By the ones I held dear

Dig at sunrise
The soil from the red lump
That shall cover me. Sow a suit mama

Acknowledge who I was
On my final lap I'll leave you a note
You the one I loved Just a plea

To take a chance at life
And I'll smile from the skies
Like the tulips that

shall decorate me
On the day I depart
And if you ever miss me
Hold dear the pages that spelt eternity

Goner series
Poetry is eternal.

AFRICAN CHILD

Carrying the weight
Pouring water on my blisters
Body aching from the day's toils
Zero balance in my accounts
Black tax weighing on me
African child
Walking barefoot in thorny fields
Hoping tomorrow will bring better dawn's
Holding on to that certificate
Sucks coz I know no one out there

African child. As destiny would have it
Living my youth Living in debt
A price I got to pay. For the failures
Of the past generations
African child. Dreams in my head
Papers under the bed
Toiling under the sun
Got taxes to pay African child
Zero pennies on me
Meanwhile its dawn's on me
The connected bird
Catches the worm

© La-ki
The tales of a poet's deepest secrets

SALI ANDIAMO SIYAYA

COUNTRY: MALAWI

ADDRESS: MACHINJIRI, BLANTYRE

WHY DO YOU WRITE POETRY?

I write poetry because it is the only way I can express my feelings

WHAT IS YOUR MESSAGE TO THE WORLD?

In everything you do, do it with love.

CHAPTER EIGHTEEN
SALI ANDIAMO SIYAYA

HERE AND NOW

Come and sing with me here and now
It's a happy tune that I have with me
Wow! Wow! Wow! you brought a cow
A great idea to celebrate with some meat
It's a happy tune that I have with me
As hungry as I am I can eat a horse
A great idea to celebrate with some meat
We will sing till our voices turn hoarse
As hungry as I am I can eat a horse

It's here and now we dance with some beer
We will sing till our voices turn hoarse
One moment here will last for a year
It's here and now we dance with some beer
For tomorrow is another song to be happy
One moment here will last for a year
I need a nappy before I can do something crappy
For tomorrow is another song to be happy
Wow, wow... you brought a cow
I need a nappy before I can do something crappy
Come and sing with me here and now.

TRACE

Take only memories leave only footprints
For nothing can disappear without a trace
Before light shuts it leaves a pint of glint

Just in case a trace of a different face
For nothing can disappear without a trace
You all have to live something behind
Just in case a trace of a different face
The good and the bad with a mysterious mind
You all have to live something behind Even

though you know that you don't know
The good and the bad with a mysterious mind
A beautiful trace that looks as white as snow
Even though you know that you don't know
The things you do on your path will follow
A beautiful trace that looks as white as snow

It's tomorrow you'll give back a borrowed sorrow
The things you do on your path will follow
Before light shuts it leaves a pint of glint
It's tomorrow you'll give back a borrowed sorrow
Take only memories leave only footprints

IF I HAD LEFT A TRACE

If only I had left a trace
Now that I am nowhere to be found
With no one along to embrace
I keep on going round and round
Now that I am nowhere to be found
I covered up my footprints so they can't
Track, I keep on going round and round

With the cracking of the ground, I can't go back
I covered up my footprints so they can't track
It's so cold and dark still I am all alone
With the cracking of the ground, I can't go back
I'm inside a stone my whereabouts are unknown
It's so cold and dark still I am all alone

To say that I'm in heaven but now it's all hell
I'm inside a stone my whereabouts are unknown
Rang me a bell tell them to wish me well
To say that I'm in heaven but now
It's all hell With no one along to embrace
Rang me a bell tell them to
wish me well If only I had left a trace.

AFRAID OF LOSING?

What are you afraid of losing?
When nothing in this world actually belongs
to you News of blues I find it amusing
Happy like a monkey caged at the zoo
When nothing in this world actually belongs
to you I decided to smile not to worry
Happy like a monkey caged at the zoo
Nevertheless, I have no stress no carry
I decided to smile not to worry

There's nothing I have, to buy anxiety
Nevertheless, I have no stress to carry
I only have myself in this society
There's nothing I have, to buy anxiety
Even depression knows that I'm broke
I only have myself in this society
Just give me a bottle of coke with some pork
Even depression knows that I am broke
News of blues I find it amusing
Just give me a bottle of coke with some pork
What are you afraid of losing?

WE WRITE POETRY

We write poetry not to make money
We write poetry because we can
We write poetry as sweet as honey

We write poetry to each and every man
We write poetry because we can
We write poetry to waste time
We write poetry to each and every man
We write poetry about crime
We write poetry to waste time
We write poetry about beautiful faces
We write poetry about crime
We write poetry to different places
We write poetry about beautiful faces

We write poetry as red as a rose
We write poetry to different places
We write poetry to propose
We write poetry as red as a rose
We write poetry as sweet as honey
We write poetry to propose
We write poetry not to make money

WE ARE THE DOGS

You make fun of us with a chicken bone
Hanging it on top so we can struggle to take
And you won't help till we get it alone
You laugh when we moan and groan
Still, we wait watching you bake the cake
You make fun of us with a chicken bone
We are the dogs under your throne
We don't participate on the rules you make
And you won't help till we get it alone
We will rise and all of yours will be gone
Since we know the friendship between us is fake
You make fun of us with a chicken bone

We are the dogs we can't be treated like clones
We have to eat thrice during daybreak

And you won't help till we get it alone
Your heart of stone is now known
We will crash it down till it breaks
You make fun of us with a chicken bone
And you won't help till we get it alone

MOTHER NATURE

Man is fighting, I will fight back
I just have to do something says Mother Nature
With his smokes I will launch an attack

He simply has forgotten the rules and law of nature
I just have to do something says Mother Nature
He's polluting air with his smokes from the chimney
He simply has forgotten the rules and law of nature
I cry for the good old days when I was with the pigmy
He's polluting air with his smokes from the chimney

Insecticides and pesticides being spread everywhere
I cry for the good old days when I was with the pigmy
All about health care but he doesn't consider my welfare
Insecticides and pesticides being spread everywhere
I was so beautiful covered in green
All about health care but he doesn't consider my welfare
Rivers, oceans and seas were so clean

I was so beautiful covered in green
I loved the way he drank from my springs
Rivers, oceans and seas were so clean
The Queen I was before he discovered benzene
I loved the way he drank from my springs
Upgraded to capturing sardines and putting them in tins
The Queen I was before he discovered benzene
Now that he cut trees and kill animals for their skins

Upgraded to capturing sardines and putting them in tins
But who will tell him that he needs discipline?
Now that he cut trees and kill animals for their skins
My adrenaline rushed for this mortal sin
But who will tell him that he needs discipline?

I will strike back Mother Nature cried
My adrenaline rushed for this mortal sin
The beautiful rivers I had have all dried
I will strike back Mother Nature cried
Giving him famine if he will not stop cutting trees

The beautiful rivers I had have all dried
Unknown diseases for him unless he says please
Giving him famine if he will not stop cutting trees
With his smokes I will launch an attack
Unknown disease for him unless he says please
Man is fighting, I will fight back

LEAVE A TRACE

It's worth to leave a good trace behind
That will continue to walk even if you stop

A trace of grace that starts with a divine mind
A good base to embrace is being kind
Lies and ego are some of the things to drop
It's worth to leave a good trace behind
Treat everyone likely even the unkind
Like on the lotus leaf life is a dewdrop

A trace of grace that starts with a divine mind
Truly great friends are hard to find
Difficult to make like a roof on a hilltop
It's worth to leave a good trace behind
As time goes clockwise it can't unwind
TICK-tock, TICK-tock on a tabletop

A trace of grace that starts with a divine mind
A good trace to bind all the mankind
They will talk about you inside a coffee shop
It's worth to leave a good trace behind
A trace of grace that starts with a divine mind

NOT YET GONE

I left a trace behind, am not yet gone
The path is all tangled and angled I can
get lost I will light up the lighter in the dark
So that you may know where to find me

I may not be in heaven I may not be in hell
If I don't get back, I left a trace for you to follow
By day by night anytime you can follow
That I may not come back if you believe am gone
I ask you to track me down I may be in hell
For the desire to see is what it cost to get lost
My heart beats louder when I see these wolves and me

It's all what I see when I am all alone in the dark
Track down my foot prints they can lead you to the dark
So-and-so there's ice below but I believe you can follow
I tried and I cried when I see what lies before me
The trace I left behind is all I have before
I be gone I'll find my way back but now
I understand that am lost And I am inside
a shell feeling as good as hell

There's a place down town that smells nothing but hell
With some holes on the wall where dogs bark in the dark
Now I'm in a hardcore show with a repetitive song of lost
Nothing I can do but to sing along and follow
I lost the lighter in a fight last night now count me gone

Am losing myself there's no way you can find me
Is there any hope, or do you have any last words for me?
Are you scared that you can't visit me in hell?
If you can't find me by dawn, then I will be gone
Nothing bright and there's no light like a spark in the dark
I read the writings on the wall and it says that you will follow
The fighting is not over yet and am not even lost
I followed a voice along the coast and now am lost

Everything is never going to be the same for me
A trace I left behind I hope you will follow
Wish a fellow well I am already in hell
But I will try as much as I can to get out of the dark
Most of my memories and everything I had is gone
Only you can get me out of this hell

I cannot live anymore alone in the dark
With a beautiful trace behind I will never be gone

GUNS AND ROSES

A gun powdered heart with deep wounds of love
It's magical you turned them into little beautiful
flowers
I will send a thousand butterflies for your everlasting beauty
A diamond heart that requires a bouquet of roses
My lady in red I am one of her smoldering secrets
And you will be mine with these smokes from my gun
A pretty rose sleeping close to a gun
Some bullets were found in the streets for her love
One son down in the chambers of her secrets
Enchanted explosive powder to cast showers of flowers

My gun looks so pretty with a magazine of roses
Straight from the army you're such a military beauty
It's a Gunner's duty to guard a malevolent beauty
My rose is shaped and truly smells like a gun
A bunch of ammunition with a fragrance of roses

Me, you, a bullet and a gun the other definition of love
With my AKA 47 I will shoot you beautiful flowers
A smith hidden under is one of our favorite secrets
A love garden guarded by a gun beneath many secrets
Spending the rest of my free time smoking beauty
A field of amulets next to a garden of flowers
I always stand closer holding nothing but a gun
My heart, my soul, feels so empty without my love
In the times of war there's no better tune than a song of roses

I stagger with these war wounds holding a bunch of roses
It takes many bullets through the heart to review these secrets
A flawless flower's fragrance attracted a dove's love

For my firearm is labeled with none other word like beauty
Too hot to touch a rose that is next to a smoldering gun
Mine is a work of art when I have to paint flowers
Blood oozing out from my chest to irrigate flowers
The reason why my field is full of red roses
Fertilizing with bullets and watering the field with a gun
So red are my roses that leave nothing but bleeding secrets
For something to be guarded and protected is all but beauty
Sent from above I made a gun for my love

A gun under a petal of red secrets that is hidden among roses
There it stays adoring the flowers' beauty A gun and a rose really fall in love

SAD SONG

It's such a sad song when she drops tears of sorrow
All she had is gone she is filled with grief
It was beautiful once but now it's all in flames
So disappointed the feeling is much more bitter
A heart of roses she was before she starts singing a sad song
She drops rain of tears down the river of pain
Filled to the brim she can't drain down the pain

A heart of roses is now covered in sorrow
She tried to remember the times she sang a beautiful song
Frozen and forgotten all she knows is grief
She once loved someone who made her life bitter
A beautiful memory was all lost in flames
She tells herself to still dance in the flames
As she will be singing a song that will soothe the pain
A cake she baked doesn't taste sweet but bitter

Looking for a happy tune all she finds is sad sounds of sorrow
Benevolently she drunk a toast to her grief
So long she cried, her salty tears salinized a colorful song
Her sharp vocals scratched the whole song
With a single match she set a melody to the flames
She drops dazzling tears to her beautiful grief
Sadly, she sang as it continues to rain in pain
Hoping for tomorrow but all she sees is sorrow
There's nothing she knows better than to say life is bitter
Hard to remake what once went bitter

Nothing she can do but singing the unforgettable song
So comfortable as she embraces herself to the sorrow
So cold she felt even standing close to the flames
She's living her life in a pretty den of pain

Such a great belief but it's all covered in grief
She looks beautiful when she dances to the sorrowful song
Like she never was jaded and bathed in something bitter
And all she hoped for was all set to the flames

THE UNDERWATER CITY

Welcome to the underwater city
Where you can only see the dark not the lights
It feels so empty and cold when the sun shines
Unfamiliar voices are heard like whispers
Where you can only see the dark not the lights
To someone living is the total nightmare
Unfamiliar voices are heard like whispers

As the scent of torture is all in the air
To someone living is the total nightmare
Screams of beautiful pain are heard everywhere
As the scent of torture is all in the air
Deep down in the sea visit us there

Screams of beautiful pain are heard everywhere
It feels so empty and cold when the sun shines
Deep down in the sea visit us there
Welcome to the underwater city

MY EARPHONES

When I put my earphones on,
I enter the world of my own
All the miseries really gone
So alone my problems unknown
I enter the world of my own
A peace I waited for so long

So alone my problems unknown
New day today my favorite song
A peace I waited for so long
I found it in my earphones
New day today my favorite song

So strong I can chew the bones
I found it in my earphones
A beautiful feeling of happiness
So strong I can chew the bones
Now that I forgot my sickness

A beautiful feeling of happiness
All the miseries really gone
Now that I forgot my sickness
When I put on my earphones

TOMBOY

I am a Tomboy
I'm here to liberate menswear
I feel nothing but joy
And am labeled with a tag of 'beware'
I'm here to liberate menswear
It's just that I don't like pink

And am labeled with a tag of 'beware'
I like my body dirty with some ink
It's just that I don't like pink
Am a Tomboy I do have some toys
I like my body dirty with some ink

And we ride just like the boys
Am a Tomboy I do have some toys
I rock with a baseball and a skateboard
And we ride just like the boys
Racing with them is easy to afford
I rock with a baseball and a skateboard
I beat boys at many things

Racing with them is easy to afford
My sneakers on they are my wings

I beat boys at many things
One bowtie at a time
My sneakers on they are my wings
Among the girls am the prime
One bowtie at a time
I wear my cap backwards
Among the girls am the prime
A champion with unknown awards

I wear my cap backwards
On a motorbike with sun glasses
A champion with unknown awards
And a genius of all classes
On a motorbike with sun glasses

I feel nothing but joy
And a genius of all classes
I am a Tomboy

DEAR MAMA

So lovely my dear Mama
For you am forever grateful
One in a million is my Mama
So beautiful yet so graceful
For you am forever grateful
Nothing is as sincerely as your kiss
So beautiful yet so graceful
Words are not enough to explain this
Nothing is as sincerely as your kiss

Like a super glue you hold the family together
Words are not enough to explain this
You are my first friend, my best friend forever
Like a super glue you hold the family together
There's no sweet word as that of a mother
You are my first friend, my best friend forever

For you are the beginning there's no one other
There's no sweet word as that of a mother
You see tomorrow when you look into my eyes
For you are the beginning there's no one other
You never slept throughout my night cries
You see tomorrow when you look into my eyes
One in a million is my Mama
You never slept throughout my night cries
So lovely my dear Mama

DEAR OCTOBER

You're the treasure of the year
I wish every month was October
So beautiful your skies are clear
Indeed, you are brilliant my beloved October
I wish every month was October
Your sun fills the world with warmth
Indeed, you are brilliant my beloved
October, I love eating scorns when it warms
Your sun fills the world with warmth
A time when leaves are turn to gold

I love eating scorns when it warms
And am told you never get so cold
A time when leaves are turn to gold
The only month I look much younger
And am told you never get so cold
Even September can't put us sunder
The only month I look much younger

You carry the season that awakens my soul
Even September can't put us sunder
So colorful you got everything in stole
You carry the season that awakens my soul
So beautiful your skies are clear
So colorful you got everything in stole
You're the treasure of the year

THE BALLAD OF M'BONA

A remarkable child of the gods
"The chosen one", some did say
To others he was so strange
He grew up within days
The legend of the rain maker
With the wind he came to a virgin lady
Who happened to be the king's sister
He was conceived without delay
Even though she really had no mister
The legend of the rain maker
After a few days he was born
For a little time in her mother's womb, he stayed
A fatherless child will never be given the throne
So many things were being told and spoke
A true legend of the rain maker
Extraordinary child he was
With the insects and flies he could play
He danced in the rain but could not get wet

It couldn't get dark unless he was done with the day
The legend of the rain maker
He turned to life what he made of clay
His little friends will run home and speak
"Mother you can't believe what happened today "
Do not tell lies", their parents will say.

DANA MICHELE SHEEHY

COUNTRY: UNITED STATES

NEW YORK

WHY DO YOU WRITE POETRY?

I write poetry to express my thoughts and feelings, in good times and bad times, in hopes that what I am thinking and feeling will be able to reach and help others. I want others to be able to feel the message that I am portraying, take that, and use it to better themselves in a way they wish.

WHAT IS YOUR MESSAGE TO THE WORLD?

There is no situation and there is no circumstance one finds themselves, in which they cannot express themselves. It is in the finding of the right words and sentences which will save your life. Communication of feelings is vital to every person to ensure a healthy state of mind and body.

CHAPTER NINETEEN
DANA MICHELE SHEEHY

THE ADVISOR

Dana Sheehy

In the streets with nothing to eat,
We finally met; I was like meat.
Begging everyone around me for drugs,
You came to me, and offered me a hug.

You drew me in with wisdom and knowledge,
And reminded me that I needed dodging.
I needed to stop chasing that high,
I needed my daughter's spirits to rise.

You gave me opportunity to talk about my dreams,
You listened to someone homeless on their knees.
I took your advice and walked to the clinic,
I never looked back,
I knew what to mimic.
I went to get help,
Which was not very hard,
Being away from my
daughter was the hard dart.

Visits are hard, as we have a great time,
We go to leave,
My daughter stops on the dime.
Give me a message in any way you can,
I do not know,
Or have a plan.

AVOID A BLOW UP

Dana Sheehy

Here we sit and there's some grit,
We have a check- in so we can spit- it.
Talking here, we listen hard,
We know what to say to be a part.

What do we say when we are feeling down?
We express ourselves healthy to avoid a frown.
Remember what we have to do,
It remembers our triggers so we can still move.

Why is it hard to walk away
from the true belittlers that can't stay away?
In the big blows where anger is high,
I remember my family avoiding that drive.

When I am targeted by anger what is it I do?
I think some deep thoughts and I gather a bit of a clue.

Try to avoid getting in arguments,
I move this way and that way to clear away heart attacks.
All of a sudden, a nice gesture is seen,
It works and a sunny day is uncovered and foreseen.
Take your time and practice ignoring words that do not pertain to you,
So, keep your head up and see how much I grew.

PROTECT MYSELF

Dana Sheehy

I'm minding my business and someone comes along,
She starts a fight and sprays nasty sauce with a prong.

Everyone hears and makes a fuss,
Ones screams at another,
Aiming her arm to throw a toss.
What I can do, to protect myself,
is mind my business, talk to others,
and look ahead to further my wealth.

Yet, my head tilts and watches the drama,
Then the dilemma thickens, Permitting the trauma.
Moving forward, I let my hair down,
I let my feet walk, my face lost the frown,
walking to town. I made it there,
and what a blear,
so many people cheered for all the happy tears.

They say I made it, without a scratch,
they say I did it, without there needing a catch.
I thought to myself, if only they knew
How much I saw and still have in view.
Let me share with you how much it takes,
To turn my head and simply walk away.

LEAVE ME ALONE

Dana Sheehy

We were friends and we had laughs,
We laughed together,
We even made crafts.

There came a point,
And it came quick,
Where your language was disgusting,
Just like a tick.

I tried to ignore it,
But it continued,
I tried to tell you,
It was just like a feud.

I asked myself,
Is this worth it?
To continue a friendship,
Or to simply split?

I wanted peace,
I wanted space,
I knew you could not provide me with grace.

So here I am, letting you know,
Our time is over,
I'm letting you go.

Please take your ammo,
Turn and leave,
You will not deny me a time to bereave.

I feel fresh,
I feel clean,
I wish I had done this when I was a teen.

I have learned that I seek peace.
I will not tolerate negativity,
Or the relationship will cease.

I feel proud and I feel great,
To take firm action in my life and in what I create.

LIVE IN ME FOREVER

Dana Sheehy

It's the time I go out,
To get some fresh air,
I'm invited to play a game,
But my heart is just not there.

I sit next to a friend,
The sun suddenly glows bright,
I feel the breeze on my cheek, still,
There's nobody to hold me tight.
A smell of a cigarette lingers,
Suddenly no wind,
I want to get up and run,
Yet there's nowhere for me to be.

I sit down to converse,
But nothing comes to mind,
I stare off at a field,
My daughter is somewhere to find.
Tears roll my cheeks,
I leave them there to feel
I remember there's a God,
One by one I kneel.

A hand touches my shoulder,
I don't look to see,
I feel the presence of something powerful,
Something that now lives in me.

AFTER THE CONVERSATION

Dana Sheehy
Dedicated to 'C'

We had one conversation
Then I knew we had
Much much more in common
Then I thought.

How would I have guessed two people
With many differences,
Had so much to talk about,
So much to discuss.

We spoke for an hour
About our similarities,
Looking each other
In our eyes
To see the shared pain,
Distrust in others,
And that's were
I found clarity.

I felt trust
In your eyes,
But that did not
Lock me in,
We laughed about
one special thing,

And with that,
I'll offer
to be your friend.

You were shy
To discuss this,
So, I did not
Burden the topic,
But it's another commonality,
Building a bridge
For this passion.

So, I won't leave you guessing,
That is simply rude,
What is our purpose in life,
After everything we do?

God is miraculous,
That's all I have to say.
I will never judge
if I have something in common
With another,
Without first having
Discussion.

RED, YELLOW, GREEN LIGHT LIFE

Dana Sheehy
Inspired by Mathew McConaughey

In life we always have strife,
But there are ways to handle it without a knife.

Let's understand some importance here,
Sometimes life will make us stop and stare.

There's another importance to talk about,
How sometimes life is okay,
Nothing to scream about,
Nothing to pout about.

Last importance life will bring,
We are doing awesome,
hitting everything that we aim.

Overall let's say it strong,
We aim for less impressed,
And go for more involved.

What exactly does this mean?
We say too much,
and the way we behave is more seen.

When life is great there are two reasons why,
It's through the choices we make,

Or it so happens to fall from the sky.

Yet let's remember,
This is life,
There will be troubles,
There will be a surprise.

This is not bad, listen please,
In order to have the great life we want,
We will need a little steam.

When making life choices,
We need to remember,
We evolve ourselves most when we are confronted or even cluttered.
Many times, in life we need to slow down,
To check the status of what is going on,
So, nothing breaks down.

There's always a chance that if we deny what's going on,
This will lead to something bad; everything will be gone.

When we are stuck in life,
And there's so much evitable strife,
We accept it for what it is,
And put down the knife.
When we admit that changes are needed to be done,
The quicker to success we are,
As well as to the fun.

Two factors to better our lives,
Always be honest,
And no shaming, to experience what is called larger than life.

Then there's times we are stuck in life,
Nobody likes this,
But it's better than being stuck in the side with a knife.

It's important for us to think about the knowledge,
we learn and use it, as if we went to college.

If we practice in trust,
We will find ourselves with a future we look forward to,
And may even lust.

There's a question in life we all have to ask,
What do we want more of in life, and also, why?

Rhythm of reflection;
Our heart and head are close again,
Reflecting honest shares and stares,
Abstain from heavy lies that fly.

Making choices and living life
comes naturally
like pen on paper
and man and wife.
When head and heart are together and configuring life.

ONE LOVELY NIGHT

Dana Sheehy

Here we are,
Talking about going far,
I've taken much,
But that's enough.

I look at you,
And you see it all,
I want to know,
How to avoid to crawl.

You seem so much at ease and peace,
The way you walk,
The way you talk.
Show me the nature of the beast,
With you I'll be at ease, then freeze.

Lying here alone at night,
Watching bats at their work, no fright.
A knock at my door, hold tight.
It's you, come in, we talk in spite.

Hour after hour, we talk at ease.
Time on our side,
Hands on our knees.
Tea is poured,
Tea is sipped.

All of a sudden, we dance and I dip.

Laughing, giggling, smiling now.
We're both hungry and say nothing at all.
3 a.m., we don't want to leave,
The cat is curled up and sleeping,
We ignore the time and deceive.

Sitting now, legs up,
Heads propped on each other,
Hands at rest.
Eyes close one by one,
The night finishes,
And they both are out done.

A GREAT DAY FOR FREE

Dana Sheehy

It's one of those days
where I feel everything will be okay,
once I go through turmoil
and see what it has to say.

There is something lurking
there in the trees,
could it be a flower,
or could it be a bee?

Let it not bother me,
let me see what it is
and if it needs help,
I will wash its wound away
So, it can be set free.

I am ready for the happy days
to wrap me up
and sing to me.
From there I go to serve the wings of others
that are less fortunate than me.

Let me open up to others
and how they can be,
As nobody is perfect,
and I can remember this

as I encourage peace.

Let nobody's intolerance get to me,
unless I ask for it to strengthen me,
and I can return the energy
and we all can glisten for free.

Let the night come in at ease,
while the sun sets,
people go to bed,
and the moon glows for free.

A MOMENT OF GREATNESS

Dana Sheehy

Have I ever felt a moment of feeling great?
Where everything around me drops under,
and I am surrounded
only by a feeling
that makes me want to celebrate?

I pause for a moment
to see if it is real,
take that moment
to look around the room
to make sure nothing has squealed.

That is when I really feel great,
that I have been acknowledged
and deserve to celebrate.

I take a deep sigh
and I'm not sure who to tell first,
of the great news of me I've heard,
or do I not tell anyone at first?

I keep smiling to myself,
and yes, people notice,
they ask,
why are you smiling,
Is there something I missed?

Inside my thoughts there's a notion
that I do want to wait for others to ask me first,
and when this happens,
I'm ready
and shout out the great news.

Then I am glowing,
as I share what greatness has been recognized,
I tell others proudly,
especially since there is nothing to be revised.
To be known for something unique
is special and the opposite of weak.
It took a long time to get there,
many many weeks.

Yes, I am proud,
as I deserve to be,
I have turned energy into greatness
and got up from my knees.

FROM DAUGHTER TO FATHER

Dana Sheehy

I have such great news
That makes me feel proud and there is no ill- use.
I have very few people to tell it to,
and you being my father,
I look to you for emotional wealth for its due.

I did a great thing here with a beautiful talent,
The response of no response from you
shows me the worth of your gallant.

It's time for a transition
where I no longer depend emotionally on you,
that when I have such great news for me,
I tug the glue off from me and you.

Will you see?
Will you bleed?
Will you wonder what it was
that made you plead?

I will share my thoughts with you,
that when I needed you most
you were simply a ghost.
I will clue you in each day it takes
and remind you of mistakes
that I swept off the plate.
Isn't this what daughters are for?
To forgive their parents
when rich or when poor?
It must be that next time
I have good news to share,

I will wait to be glee
for the times the streets are calling me.

All I yearn for
are more special moments,
of when my dad is proud
of his daughter without a notion.
Giving me hugs
when I didn't expect it,
telling me words
that he is proud which
he wants to admit it.

I will be okay
if I do not reach his expectations.
That my great news is nothing
but a shake of the hand.

This does not reflect
any character of mine.
These words and behaviors
belong to my dad,
for him to shine.
He taught me well
that limitations will only
get me feeling fine.

I taught myself
that if I want to go further in life
I will always be great
when others' responses
to what I do are simple,
and there will be no bother to me
in the middle of the night.

LISTENING TO OTHERS

Dana Sheehy

How is it that I end up with others,
that I have nothing in common with,
while sipping my coffee.

I want to talk about the job culture,
I want to know about education for the younger,
While others are too busy talking about spending their money,
about what pants they will buy,
about what makeup will hide.
How do I connect with the women that are opposite than I?

Will I pretend that I care about these things
that help just themselves and not another person trying?
Yes, fashion is fun,
but above all,
It does not interest me at all.

Shall I share what my thoughts are?
I make one comment about the job market,
and everyone stands and starts to walk out.

Maybe it is not all the women that surround me that are exactly like this,
that have nothing in common with me,
and there are others around me who care about
the commonwealth of a child and who have more bliss.

Next suggestion is that I move out a bit further.
My current surroundings are too much closed in,
and this is why I am not able to find any like- minded friends.

So let me go deep and find more attributes,
that I can bond with others with,
and take the blame out,
to make a new connection.

I am sweet,
I am neat,
I like to talk,
I like to learn,
and with no concern.

So, then I have my new found friend,
and we go about the community,
talking from end to end.

MY FIRST MEETING WITH LIKE MINDED PEOPLE

Dana Sheehy

I find you people with the internet,
We all come together,
there's nothing to break from a bet.
We all are looking for the same renewal,
That's within our life and within our soul.

We reach out to each other,
to get the solution that will fix one another.
It's within our souls that lets us unite,
We each have a piece to contribute that brings out the daylight.
We all have to speak to let the message spread,
So, we all can listen and say grace in the end.

Let everyone be open to receive the serenity,
This is the gift that we all gather together
and helps us choose our identity.
Let no questions be asked when the time comes and the gift appears,
For beauty, elegance, and wisdom all in one presents
and has no fears.
How will you welcome the new found gift?
Will you be open- minded to be honest, respectful, and accept this without a twist?
Will you accept there is a God that lives amongst us?
That God has saved us so many times, and now there is a new found trust.
The group has helped me lead me to God, and I was able to open up.

A LUXURY SURPRISE

Dana Sheehy

I do not deserve what is about to come,
Such a great time with a man, with a beautiful outcome.
Just knowing we will meet is enough for me,
No fancy meal resulting in a large fee.

Should we do coffee for our first 'date',
A magnificent surprise of how good we relate.
Do I dare jinx this and call this a date from the gate?
I see the hearts that come from his heart,
I see the genuine messages that are sent, never far apart.

The time of my life awaits me ahead,
Do I dare tell him and leave a hint that's a shred?
The fear of rejection is there at the forefront,
I do not dare scare him,
by telling him the feelings I have in my heart
and in my head.
I will enjoy the time and his presence he will share.
I will tell him the things about me, which he would like to hear.
When he smiles I will too,
there's no way on this day I will turn blue.
Will he think of me when we leave?
Will he want to see me another day?
Already thinking about day two,
As I lay here thinking about the luxury of day one
and how I will get through.

IT TAKES A VILLAGE

Dana Sheehy

There was a boy who was a fright,
His clothes were ripped and he frowned in the night.
He was six and didn't know his parents.
He cried all the time looking for them with perseverance.

He lived in a town called Helick,
Where everyone knew him for looking for food,
but instead he got dietetic.
Nobody wanted him and yet knew he needed a place.
So, he went bouncing from home to home,
Visiting like a relative from outer space.

He begged and pleaded at every home,
To please be let in, he would moan and moan.
He offered to do chores, he used his manners,
Still, nobody budged, he even lit their lanterns.

Over the days he prayed and prayed.
He went to the priest in which they did offerings of the word and layed.
He went to each house, willing to do their biddings,
The families agreed to his use, then kicked him out until it was time for fillings.

He needed some music so he sang songs to himself,
He moped around the streets until he found another chore for an elf.

He thought to himself, where are my parents, why did they leave me, is this apparent?
The priest was sad and told him one day, his parents were killed by mobsters from Clay.

The boy now knew why nobody wanted him,
The people of Helick were afraid of protecting him.
Here he was doing their chores,
Here he was not even being adored.

So, the boy decided to stick up for himself.
To leave the town, and go somewhere where he can be proud.

MY BOW

Dana Sheehy

I move on to better things,
I progress to show I can fly with wings.
My head is up, my eyes are open,
My feet are steady, my arms wide open.

There I go, on to Phase 2,
But where is my family?
They believed I wouldn't come through.
I'm looking back for my support,
I see nothing of assort.
I trip up and hurt my knees,
Some tears fall down,
But then I breathe.

I tell myself to get back up,
Don't let them win,
Don't or I'll blow up.
So, I get up on my own,
I keep walking,
And refrain from a moan.
There's someone I love,
Who needs me now,
I'll never give up for her,
She deserves my bow.

IT'S A SPIRIT NIGHT

Dana Sheehy

It's a cloudy day, the people are gloomy and in a daze.
The kids want to trick or treat, to gather candy, to be something neat.
The candy is delicious and the candy is sweet.
The parents are fixing the costumes to portray some deceit.

A bang at the door, the kids run, there's nothing there, there's nothing to be done.
This must be a trick in the air.
The kids go out for nothing but more dares.

Trick or treat are heard throughout.
You see a ghoul; you see many freaks out.

The lights go out throughout the 'hood.
Everybody stopped, they wanted to run, but nobody could.
Another trick, you hear so loud,
Why it's a spirit that lurks there now.

I'm here to make your night a fright,
I'm here to scare you good, all right.

What do you want? Calls a parent.
I want your spirit of Halloween, it's transparent.
I want your candy and your spirit!
Let me have it, you better hear it.
I will make your kids give me their laughs,

I will make you children run into a gap.
The parents were mad and didn't know what to do.
They said no way, just look at you!
A little girl comes up to the spirit,
Invites it to their home and says it can live near it.

The spirit stopped and thought about this.
It asked if it can laugh and smile with the little girl named Chris?
She said yes, she wouldn't mind, and the spirit turned the lights back on, so no more fright.

WHEN YOU LEAVE

Dana Sheehy

My dear daughter, there you go.
We just visited, and tears just roll.
I put ourselves in this position,
Now I have to ask to see
you with permission.

The pain I feel when you leave,
It is so much, I simply grieve.
The people around me smile and laugh,
While here I am simply aghast.

I want you back with me now.
The tears just roll,
I will get you with me,
somewhere, somehow.

I feel your pain in the long hugs,
I see the agony in your eyes when we talk.
Feeling you when you are on my lap,
Makes me free, makes me trapped.

What do I say when it's time for you to go?
Of course, that I love you, yet,
That I messed up months ago?
Please forgive me before you go.

I cannot live, without this,
It seems my life is going so slow.
Months go by, and months will come,
And then we will live together at once.
Our hearts will beat together just like before,
You, my daughter, is the only thing I adore.

THE THERAPIST

Dana Sheehy

You sit there in my office,
Writing notes all of the judgment.
Tilting my head,
Wondering then,
Who is this I am confronting?

Is she worth the time?
Is she worth a dime?
I have no clue to really say,
All I remember are her crimes.

Is she of any value?
What does she really gather?
When we talk and she listens,
At the end of the conversation will she glisten?

Does this person really care?
Does she care about what she will bare?
She has the strength; Will she go the length?
Will she let me save her at full length?

She looks at me so pleasantly,
She smiles there with what seems, so much care, so much glee.
She laughs without a hesitation,
Never looking at her watch for the duration.

In that much time, Now I see,
It's me that needs the therapy.
I need to laugh, I need to smile,
Yet I am here judging others all the while.

DAHLIA CONSTANT

COUNTRY: PHILIPPINES

WHY DO YOU WRITE POETRY?

I write poem to describe my feeling , the life cycle, memories, and nature.

Every pieces of poem is parted of my dreary tears".

CHAPTER TWENTY
DAHLIA CONSTANT

AT NIGHT

This night is dark; nothing I seen has light .
This night is lonely without pouring love.
This night is filled with silence and
broken smiled , I hope everything will be alright .

This night without stars and no yellow light
I look through sadness smile's .
This night I see the moon whole and brighter
And never leave me this, moment are questionable .
Don't tell to me a sweet healer words
To covered your worse .
Don't say that you are my savior

That's, when I need someone everyone
Left me unknown.
Don't say anything because , I'm not audience
your sister doesn't deserve to hear a
Sweetness lie words .

MY LOVE

Hold my hand oh dear love ,
I wish your the last man
that I could dance .
From the daylight through the dark
Don't leave, stay by my side
Until the sunrise comes up
Don't let away your hand
Holding me tight .

We will go wherever place we want,
We will play, and laugh
until the history stayed our heart.
Let's cherish this moment
my pleasure love
Take me to Paris and
let us dance ;
Without any audience
can caught
Make it private , in our

hearts that always beat .
I could not stop this ..
I should not done this..
I'm still seeking you ;
wherever place I through ...
Your my king under
the dark and Brighter light .
And we will make a thousand
smile and endless cries
By cheering our love story
starts in glance.

~ D.C

SUFFER BY PAST

At the right time I will knock .
I open my heart and spoke,
Where my eyes, already blindfold.
Through the dark surround.

Nowhere , I heard the past
Ruin my better future .
Through heaven , through hell
Each of them I choose only one way.

~ D.C

AT THE WINDOW

At the window nearly on my bed.
Where my sister starts to think
By staring the clouds and thinking on how.

At the window surrounded with dark
I hope before she left, she didn't take
This bed looks like slavery place.

At the window without holiday are like
November months, any time is Dead heart
and numb, filled with broken heart.

At the window I glance the view, it seems
Has many clues, and I found a knew
with using Pen descripting I missed someone here.

At the window where so many tears dry
And dreary glad, I ate the bitterness
While some killed their sweetness.

At the window I nearly I sit near on my bed.
Where I count the day, I passed and a day
When you starting to lose my side.

Wrote by: " D.C

CLOSE YOUR EYES

Close your eye
I will tell you why?
Close your eye
And yell all you seen high
Close your eye
And imagine I'm nearly
by your side.
Close your eye
And blink one time.
Close your eye
And asked me why?
Close your eye
You will see how dark
surround if no light around.
Close your eye
And imagine, that all people you love
Nearly hold your hand. and tells it's alright '
Close your eye
And few minutes you can sleep and
thankful if you wake and that's a gift.
Close your eye
What kind color compared
in your inner side.
Close your eye
And you feel a peace of
mind with control
in the situation messing all around.

Close your eye
Because, I'm here by your side
and still looking you all apart.
Close your eye
By waiting the moment that happened you and I
Close your eye
And realized, how pleasure the moment
When he did not leave you in your sight
Close your eye
Not your heart I will knock and comeback
Don't say it's too late. when I heard my name
While you wait.
Close your eyes.
While waiting our paths to meet
And you my gifted desire.

Wrote by ~ D. C

DEATH

I asked for death.
what's the meaning of each,
Death Did not replied; And
possibly comes
In the right time,
When I am ready
To say goodbye'
Death is gift.
For those people
immediately received
And misery that I
Couldn't accept.

Death is happened
entire on whole world
Without knowing
what date it's happened
Could tomorrow or evening be ready
In anytime and anywhere?
people leave by their own timeline
A death known as R.I.P that possibly
No one' can escape this nightmare
None of entire human left,
this world filled nothing can take.

Wrote by: " D.C

EVENING TEARS

I sat down on a chair and,
falls my tears;
Without knowing
what happening?
I Declared me
self-slave in pain
Evening moments
that makes me cry
harder and screaming
like losing everything
and nothing seems again.

Wrote by: " D.C

BEHIND THE MASK

How wonderful you see
Beautiful smiles on me,
With full of scar's,
With my past,

Even words
Can't heal my soul,

I'm not tolerant
I got damage
on my scar's,
Who makes me
different a man,
I see a house
not a home,
I feel I'm alive
with pain inside,

I cried not enough,
Every day at night,
How many friends
Do I have,
I don't know
Where I'll be knock?

I looked the window
Everything is locked I see moon shining

Alone the dark, Behind of mask
I wear any time, Make up smile
Can see society
I feel alright, I'm like a dust

Blinding anyone with my smile,
I'm like a shadow I'll be your side
But invisible When you
walked forward,

How pain I paint Will kill myself,
Even pen describe My problem,
Behind of mask You can lie
But now adays
Someone understands
Your pain ...

Wrote by: " D.C

MORNING POEMS

A wonderful day, I woke up And I see the light.
With brightly colors that I wish I had.
In morning daylight, God saved me in the dark.
Through the light I see the reality that woke up
My mind in places where I settle and hide.

Wrote by: " D.C

SPRING SEASONS DAY

I lost the gleam;
for gave a flower gloom.
Every morning rise in their time zone.
With sun apparent in sky.
On spring seasons day.
That Glamorize those people
to bring a beautiful smile.
With Flogging wind at spring days
That those people felt like
It's a new chapter verse.

Wrote by: " D.C

DARKEST LIFE

Life is short, haven't got such good memories
Life experience found in stupidity things
Life is betrayal found in backstabber
Life is meaningless, if you found you alone in this earth.
Life turned to mess if you serious about challenge.
Life is a song, it can describe any worse situations
Life is misery when you feel lonely
Life is blind, if you realized all is temporary and leave you behind.
Life is darker, if you don't know
Who's yourself.

Wrote by: " D.C

GIVE ME A REASON

Give me a reason to live?

Give me a reason to stayed?

Give me armor to face this challenge?

Give me peace at point 0f mess happens?

Give me the missing part of Puzzle of my heart?

Give me a word alright when I can't survive?

Give me a reason to not quit this journey?

Give me strength when I feel doubting in morning?

Give me best hug with looking my eyes and tells "are you alright."

Give me the light, I can't see because I'm cage of dark?

Give me the song that' makes me feel not alone?

Give me a rose's not in funeral but roses of true love really mean?

Give a word that describe my reflection?

Give me a place that's I truly belong?

Give faith with lied promise broke me into pieces?

Give the life?

"I really truly feel alive"

D. C

LONELY NIGHT

Lonely night one man carried bag
Went through the darker house.
With, Yellow constant Light.
Makes her home brighter
by Surrounding with shining yellow might
Man remembered his moment_
With somebody lost by her side_
And, In every blow of winds
Her mind takes him to the moment
Memories, that he can't let go and survive.
That' make's him felt sad in one moment
of night, that man needs hug.

D.C

----- WAY

Way to __ left

Way to __ right

There' is no easy

In first _ step.

Look forward

Or look back

Everything

Will going to

Be alright.

Noisy or silent

Everyone Have a

Mouth To speak --

Darkside Or

Bright side Everyone

Has them Time to

Live, what?

Places they like.

LAST WISH

Would you cry,
if I'll die?
Would you visit my grave,
when you have a time?
Would you give me flowers,
and light my candles?
Would you sit for awhile
and tell about your day?

And if one day,
I'll be gone.
Would you miss me?
would you remember my name?
Would you share some stories
and silly things about me?

And if my body becomes weak and cold,
and my heart beat will stop.
As you see my eyes close,
please, don't bother to wake me up.

Please, let me. Let me be free,
from painful heartaches
and misery.

Let me see the light again,
let me feel that I'm alive again.

Let me aim the liberty.
from hidden dark past,
and uncurable curse.

Let me sleep on serenity
Let me leave peacefully.
I just want to be happy.
And live in a faraway place.

"Her Thousand Thoughts"
Do you believe that everything
will ends? including you.

Have you ever known
that one day you will
die? and one day,
no one will remember
you, your name, something
facts about you.

That's the saddest but truth.
We will all leave in this world.
Because this is only stages,
where all of us are a player.
We are just only a caretaker
not the owner. It tells we don't
have rights to own everything
we have. It's just a temporary
to test the faith, we had.

Be fair and equal. Even royal
will bow to their superior.
Pride won't save you
to the river of fire but your purity,
kindest and faithfulness
it can. money, fame, popularity,
properties and even your trophies
can't do it. It's just only a material thing
not a source. If you a wise
person, you will understand
each phrase.

So, tell me. 'What would you be doing now?'
So, until we have a time, let's cherish, treasure
and enjoy the moment we have in this
world. Please remember this, this is not
the real world we thought, this is just
a test world where we will be screen,
if we have a right to live in paradise
where forever is beyond than we thought.

D.C

SARAH OTIENO

COUNTRY: KENYA

WHY DO YOU WRITE POETRY?

Sarah Otieno is a poetry lover. My interest in poetry came after meeting my best friend who is a writer, Lavin Owende, reading her work motivated me to do more. My writings happen to be an expression of my emotions, whenever I am on low no one to talk to, my pen and paper talk to me. My dream is that one time my art work be known worldwide and encourage people going through something.

CHAPTER TWENTY-ONE
SARAH OTIENO

EMPTY SOUL

My life's like a ladder
Once used no one cares
Only needed when it's beneficial
My life was once divine
When my smile was honest
Loving one and only... momma
So, like a dream

Waking up to face the reality
Momma got herself free
I cry for what I feel inside
Physical pain seems better than this
I crave and long for her like crazy
And it hurts really bad
That I still miss and love her

It's going to hurt me to hate you
But loving you is worse
You don't care about a thing
Throwing away what we share just like that
We didn't just invest time in it...
Emotions were as well involved
Honestly, you're nothing like the OG momma.

MOM

Nine months is not a joke
Carrying me in your womb
Without abortion thoughts
The morning sickness, allergies and vomiting
Am grateful for you mama
You're my number one hero
Brest feeding me when starving
Protecting me from evil eyes
Changing my diapers
Washing my mess with no complain
You're such a loving mother
You're my number one hero

Every woman is a super hero
It takes one with motherly ability
To take the responsibility of a child
And no one teacher is always mama
My mom, my heart
You're my number one hero

By just guessing in my eyes
You already knew what I needed
You embraced me with love and tenderness
You made sure I become your number one priority
You're my humanly God
You're my number one hero.

LOVE IS....

Love is like a rose If not well taken care of
It withers and dies. A perfect rose requires;
Patience and watering, so is love
Patience and watering, by watering
That's where loyalty, understanding comes in

Love is like a candle Lits brightly
But when in a windy environment
You have to do all it takes to make it firm
And never goes off

Love is like lemon Bitter when eaten raw
Sweet in lemonade form Just like lemon, for sweet love
You have to spice it up

Love is sweet and sour Depending on who you love
If you get yourself one who loves you for you
You're complete
The one who don't value your worth or opinion
You're finished
And finally, the one who loves your money
You're completely finished.

PROCRASTINATION

It's the nature of our political leaders
Coming up with very sassy seducing agendas
To seduce voters during campaigns
Agendas such as, free education
When some of us still have their certificates held
For fee arrears

Jobs for the youths
When graduates are burning their papers
Claiming they have no use
Good life style, while the rich get richer
And the poor gets poor
It's just political games

After election, is when the reality play
A mere ward representative locating to the city
Leaving his/her ward to be ruled by who?
Things on the ground got hit up
The once suffering are the voters
Especially once who sold their votes

They sit on their fancy chairs and forget about us
When we complain about high cost of living
Reduction of goods prices but increase taxation
They take as they give it's a win win for them
They introduce subdues to calm us
So that they buy time

With the politician it's never easy in my country
I suggest this land be sold
Everyone be paid
So that we can live with no expectations
Coz every president with fake promises
And it's us who suffer
Vision 2030 is around the corner
Don't be shocked if it's postponed to 2050

During campaigns, politicians are like men in love
A man in love can promise you the whole world
But once you give in and say yes
The whole world turns into a small house in the village
Not even a city
Your vote, your choice
Vote wisely.

I SAW A DEMON

Come all Lemme show you
It's a real demon
Whose features resemble mother Mary
Not until you get in her circle
You won't notice a thing It's not just me
But many describe demons to be
Having horns and bloody mouth
But it's just a myth we were told at tender age
To scare the hell out of us
We got it all wrong, description of a demon
I got cuffed in different chains
All I could praise was me being in love
Little did I know my energy was drained
Bit by bit
"I LOVE YOU MORE," was a daily chorus
Me and my crazy heart fell for every word
I was such a nincompoop
That's when Nicki's line hit my ears
People will love you only when it's beneficial
As soon as I was of no use The love was gone
It's better dealing with the demon you know
than the angel you know nothing about
Not all that beauty symbolizes angel
Some demons pose in beauty to attract
Be warned!!!!

SPARE ME MOMMA

For now, spare me momma
Don't ask me to love another
How can I trust another after this?
Let me take it one step at a time
Lemme nurse my wounds
Collect the broken pieces
And I promise to fulfil your wish
Once these obsessions seem to have ceased
And when I have learnt about love again
The whole universe shall know
Not only you dear... that am finally ready
Ready to love again
There will be no turning back
No retreat no surrender
But I'll put me first all through
No more loving someone more than myself

EMPTY SOUL

My life's like a ladder
Once used no one cares
Only needed when it's beneficial
My life was once divine
When my smile was honest
Loving one and only... momma
So, like a dream

Waking up to face the reality
Momma got herself free
I cry for what I feel inside
Physical pain seems better than this
I crave and long for her like crazy
And it hurts really bad
That I still miss and love her

It's going to hurt me to hate you
But loving you is worse
You don't care about a thing
Throwing away what we share just like that
We didn't just invest time in it...
Emotions were as well involved
Honestly, you're nothing like the OG momma

SENSATIONAL

The heart is heavy as lead
Filled with tears not shed
Covered with demonic emotions
Straining and creating indecisions
Bitter tears scalding the eye
So, they swam in pool of ice

Love is not all about laughter and joy
It can be cold .... really cold
Heart bleeding and pleading inside
Feelings and desires that seems not to cease
One walks upside down, hands astride
The inside love on the outside

The far have got...love I beg
Do not sting me...Let me be
I want to be happy, am never meant for love
For in love my energy is drained
Lossing myself for one who never
Appreciate my worth.

ACKNOWLEDGEMENTS

No effort of this magnitude gets accomplished without the finest efforts from several people. First on the list is Theophilus Agbu Clement, also known as "Theo." He was responsible for putting together the entire book and coordinating the countless meetings. Theo walked this trail with me from start to finish. He knows my heart and my mind. He was always there for me researching, editing, or hosting zoom calls. Theo was especially gifted at knowing what I needed when I needed it including encouragement to continue pressing on or offering to do more than he was already doing. This book would not have happened without Theo, and I am eternally grateful to him for taking this journey with me.

To my author's representative Francesca Maria, you were there for me when I published my own book and here you are again supporting me. Thank you for being you and always being there for me.

To the contributing twenty-one poetesses, a heartfelt thank you for trusting me with your work. May this book long be a source of pride for both you and your families. Please hold this book close to your heart and know that your voice matters. You are the creators of sending positive ripples into the universe. May the blessings of the universe be upon you and your family both now and forever.

CONTACT INFORMATION

Promoter and Producer: Blair N. Smith;
Blairsmith0505@gmail.com

Editor and Coordinator: Theophilus Agbu Clement;
clementtheophilus4@gmail.com

www.ingramcontent.com/pod-product-compliance
Lightning Source LLC
LaVergne TN
LVHW061531070526
838199LV00027B/603/J